THE HÖLDERLINIAE

A POEM

ALSO BY NATHANIEL TARN

POETRY

Gondwana, 2017
The Persephones, 1974, (rewritten) 2008, 2016
The Beautiful Contradictions, 1969, 2013
Ins and Outs of the Forest Rivers, 2008 • *Avia*, 2008
Recollections of Being, 2004 • *Selected Poems: 1950–2000*, 2002
Three Letters from the City: The St. Petersburg Poems, 2001
The Architextures, 2000 • *The Architextures 1–7*, 1999
A Multitude of One (editor: poems by Natasha Tarn), 1994
Flying the Body, 1993
Caja del Río, 1993 • *The Army Has Announced that Body Bags . . .*, 1992
Home One, 1990 • *Seeing America First*, 1989
The Mothers of Matagalpa, 1989 • *At the Western Gates*, 1985
The Desert Mothers, 1984 • *Weekends in Mexico*, 1982
The Land Songs, 1981 • *Atitlán/Alashka* (w. Janet Rodney), 1979
Birdscapes, with Seaside, 1978
The Forest: from Alashka (w. Janet Rodney), 1978
The Ground of Our Great Admiration of Nature: from Alashka (w. Janet Rodney), 1977
The Microcosm, 1977 • *The House of Leaves*, 1976
Lyrics for the Bride of God, 1975 • *Section: The Artemision*, 1973
A Nowhere for Vallejo, 1971 • *The Silence*, 1969 • *October*, 1969
Where Babylon Ends, 1969
Selection: Penguin Modern Poets 7, 1965 • *Thirteen for Bled*, 1965
Old Savage/Young City, 1964

TRANSLATIONS

The Penguin Neruda, 1975 • *The Rabinal Achi*, Act 4, 1973
Con Cuba, 1969 • *Stelae* (Segalen), 1969 • *Selected Poems* (Neruda), 1968
The Heights of Macchu Picchu (Neruda), 1966

PROSE

The Embattled Lyric: Essays & Conversations in Poetics & Anthropology, 2007
Scandals in the House of Birds: Shamans & Priests on Lake Atitlán, 1998
Views from the Weaving Mountain: Selected Essays in Poetics & Anthropology, 1991

THE HÖLDERLINIAE

A POEM

Nathaniel Tarn

A NEW DIRECTIONS PAPERBOOK ORIGINAL

Portrait of Friedrich Hölderlin by F. K. Hiemer, c. 1792

First published as a New Directions Paperbook (NDP1496) in 2021
Manufactured in the United States of America
Design by Eileen Bellamy

Library of Congress Cataloging-in-Publication Data
Names: Tarn, Nathaniel, author.
Title: The Hölderliniae : a poem / Nathaniel Tarn.
Description: First edition. | New York : New Directions Books, 2021. | "A New Directions Paperbook original"
Identifiers: LCCN 2020043312 | ISBN 9780811230636 (paperback | ISBN 9780811230698 (ebook)
Subjects: LCSH: Hölderlin, Friedrich, 1770–1843—Poetry.
Classification: LCC PS3570.A635 H65 2021 | DDC 811/.54—dc23
LC record available at https://lccn.loc.gov/2020043312

10 9 8 7 6 5 4 3 2 1

New Directions Books are published for James Laughlin
by New Directions Publishing Corporation
80 Eighth Avenue, New York 10011

ndbooks.com

*A Requiem to the Immortal Memories of my
Elders Friedrich Hölderlin & Susette
"Diotima," his Beloved; also to my
Younger Co-Pilot Fryderyk Chopin ---*

Together with the Beethoven of the Last Quartets.

Also for two Beloved Sisters: P.R.T. & J.R.T.

BIOGRAPHICAL NOTE

Friedrich Hölderlin was born in 1770 at Lauffen on the Neckar River in Swabia, Württemberg, Southwestern Germany with a later move close by to Nürtingen. His father died when he was two and a second father died when he was nine. He often spoke later in life of a long-lasting double grief. His mother, followed by siblings, ruled over him all his life, holding back the money and resources he needed to live as a poet. She saw him becoming a vicar or parish priest under the Lutheran Pietist Consistory that oversaw the lives of a great many in the Swabian elite. That path, as seen by society, involved a first assistantship, a probable marriage to the vicar's daughter and then the vicariate itself.

Hölderlin began school in 1776, receiving additional tuition in Greek, Hebrew and Latin. He formed a friendship with the future philosopher Friedrich Schelling, an associate for most of his life. In 1784, Hölderlin entered a second, ecclesiastical school to start his training into the Lutheran ministry. He discovered the poetry of Friedrich Klopstock and Friedrich Schiller and took his own tentative steps in verse, avidly pursuing his literary interests. It is here that his doubts about the ministry are said to have started to surface. In 1778 he began theological studies proper at the Tübingen *Stift*, a theological seminary where fellow students included Schelling, Hegel and Isaac von Sinclair: these figured prominently in his later life. They and other young men were budding republicans, passionately interested in the French Revolution, wondering whether it would ever reach Germany. Though hating the Terror, interest continued when the young Napoleon stunned them with his military victories. Hölderlin declared his wish to leave the *Stift* to study law, but this move was scotched by his mother.

After obtaining his degree, Hölderlin took the one main permitted way to avoid the ministry: working as a private tutor to young children, a difficult life in regard to the social status of the teacher, never knowing if he were a servant or a guest. In 1794 he met Schiller—at first a magisterial and idolized protector—together with Goethe, and began writing his "novel" *Hyperion*. In 1795 he enrolled for a while at a major intellectual center, the University of Jena, attending the philosophical lectures of Johann Gottlieb Fichte and meeting many other prominent faculty and students including another great poet: Novalis.

As a tutor in Frankfurt from 1796 to 1798, he and Susette Gontard, the wife of his employer, a businessman, fell passionately in love. Whether there was an affair in the full sense or not seems rarely if at all to have been discussed but this was the most important relationship in Hölderlin's life. The matter being discovered; the poet was dismissed and lived in Homburg until 1800, not too far away to prevent difficult clandestine meetings.

Here he produced his most important poems, the great *Hymns*, as well as three versions of a tragedy: *The Death of Empedocles*. But he suffered immensely from the loss of his Diotima (the name he gave Susette) and from what most authorities believe was a decline in his mental state leading eventually to acute Schizophrenia. One fervent scholar, Pierre Bertaux, has argued in vast detail against "madness" proper and for a permanent profound depression leading eventually to the poet's acceptance of a hermit's existence for the last half of his life. Attempts by Hölderlin over this time to find literary avenues for making a living failed: this very much due to his famous friends' tacit refusal to help him, in short to their desertion.

After a sojourn in Stuttgart at the end of 1800 while he worked on his translations of Pindar, Sophocles and other Greek classics—derided without understanding by Schiller and others—he held tutorships in Switzerland and in France, at Bordeaux, the latter in 1802, returning home to Nürtingen totally exhausted and eventually learning of Susette's death. After two years trying to continue work at home, including constant changes and emendations to the poems (making their study hugely difficult) his friend Von Sinclair found him an honorary job as a Court Librarian. A variety of personal, very conflictual and political problems between a number of friends, eventually caused Sinclair to advise Hölderlin's mother to treat him as a failed citizen and a scandal to Pietists. She moved him—kidnapped him, some maintain—to a clinic for the mentally ill in Tübingen. Hölderlin's treatment was drastic and horrible. After a couple of years, he was released and given three years to live. A cultured (he knew the *Hyperion*) master carpenter, Ernst Zimmer, and his family took him in and gave him the most loving care he had ever received. His family continued to wrangle over his patrimony—which would have made him rich well before—and did not visit him. He continued to write simple poems, very different from his greatest work, and received visitors, amicably or not, in the *Turm*, the tower of Zimmer's house overlooking the Neckar. It is now known as the *Hölderlinturm*, a museum. He stayed there thirty-six years until his death, aged 73, in 1843.

It took a hundred years for Hölderlin to be recognized not only as a great, perhaps the greatest German poet but as the First Modern Poet to many cultures in the twentieth century and beyond.

THE HÖLDERLINIAE

A POEM

It is a question of a murder: a man is murdered wishing
to live a life *He's* not allowed to lead over two hundred
years ago. *He* wished to be a poet. His folks wanted a
clergyman. *He* fought long, hard and, at the end, *He* lost
his mind. A question then of being murdered, of being
slowly murdered. By life which turns to death as birds
drop sky to ground, at faint of gnat biting your cheek.

While sky falls into trees, trees fall to ground, ground
falls to lake and lake into the deepest ocean, for which
the gods -- those mirrors of our fates decked out in blue
evaporating coral -- will never raise themselves to gather
back the sky. *And/Und & But/Aber*: impossible to see,
to witness gods in high sky shining down on where
one lives because that domicile is being murdered also.

In sleepless nights before dead fires, assassinated fires:
no coming up for air, no pass from worm to fish, from
fish to ape, from ape to --- what! this *thing* is human?
this thing debased, massacred, gassed and paralyzed,
ghost-like legions of murdered men: when wars decide
never to end, never to terminate, when wars begin again
at cap drop, enter our lungs: we can no longer breathe.

It is a question of being murdered day by day, night after
night with not a single breathing space between a sleep
and sleep, become the one escape, the only right royal
residence left in the universe -- and sleep turns into death
without a warning. Which hey! is being murdered, ended
just like *He* was by loss of sanity, by loss of mind, by
golden girl dying of death: what else -- the bitter husband?

Among great Hymns, Odes, Elegies, and Fragments: *He*
spoke it first, wrote of it first, "*Mich reizt der Lorbeer. Ruhe
beglückt mich nicht*" / "It is the laurel that I want, not peace
and quiet." Singer of rivers reversing time: if there's a single

drop of life left in this man, this man is being slowly murdered: it is become of him, because he lived and died among the dying peoples, the deaf, the paralyzed, the gods.

Death has a thousand cards to play. Life only one.

The lives that are being lived, the lives out there
that are being lived -- we know not one entirely,
not even just a part, one breath in the mountain
air or the lowland air, one wish, one small desire,
infinitesimal, footloose below those heights, and
so followed we are, trapped and condemned to
these existences in the below. And how was it in
those days then, those days so deeply buried, what
were those others, those we call "lives" what were
they doing in this apparent motion, let's say this
                    semblance of a life?

There is a being sitting next to us, a being ardent,
so packed with thoughts, wishes, desires and fears
it would take whole new inner "lives" to read, to
comprehend. Multiply this by millions, reach down
into the lower lives, the seabed lives, reach up into
the upper lives, cloud lives and tempest lives and
lives lived in the winging blue between the clouds -
when cloud-filled skies then empty out and there is
nothing but the blue to wing one's way through and
                    to cover heads:

Those of the wondering, to fill those heads with
Oh! the information that we'll never read and never
understand, (not that the past was understood, not
that the present is, not that the future ever will be)
and we'll be left so thoroughly alone, we'll be in
danger of never waking up, we'll be so certain that
we were born depressed, that, from the start, there
was a floor of sadness we never could dig down to,
and that whatever would desire to fill a space over
the floor would lack in purity, would fail to mark,
to manifest or fathom any happiness, would be the
            angel of destruction over any love.

Poet now lover has a pit he cannot fill and must look
upward to those blue skies in which to find the naked
likeness of a goddess living there that can make him
a god. *He* does not know: he cannot reach that. The
multiplicity can only weigh him down. How now, this
very day among our days to make that incalculable fair
number reach into one, become a one? It must become
has to become the one and then that one will in its turn
form part of multiplicity and there's no end to searching.
Cannot be made in any sense into coherence. For that
fair plural will itself become again part of the him up
in her bosom. *She* has now abdicated her own divinity
in joining him -- and all they own today is this -- Oh!
loving life illuminates duration. We have thought ever,
endlessly, day after day, trying to reach that one beloved.
She we have found. Now there is hardly nothing left at
all except to die.

Hard to remember. The joy of it, the ecstasy. The endless
peering at that face, the one and only face now re-defined
as "Beauty." Oh! Blissful creature! *She* stands there: in the
ruins of ages. And there, right there, we stand, right there,
we are. We have become. The sense that this, once found,
is yes, indeed, the goddess. The "*She*" will fill this life and,
why not think it? May even walk well far beyond this life
into whatever may be said to become after. Nature has now
reached down into the leaves, the flowers, the crops, the sea,
the rivers marching to break infinity, the skies above them
shining down into the waters and filling them with life, a
smiling life, a laughing life to flavor all our days, to cushion
them into old age. The life is sung at last, a singing satisfies,
there is not even need of any listener. However, it would do,
it would do splendidly if there were some assembly, some one
community in which we would delight with love spread far
and wide over the earth. Yes, they would grow in time and
flourish, not leaving us behind. We do adore it.

An insufficiency of language. An excess of language.
The long years studying a language *I* do not use. The
subjects of discussion are of no interest. *I* am / *I* am not.
He: going back to mother -- again, again. *I*, attempting
to explain huge spider on the curtain as *I* wake shortly
after birth -- from out the crib. Explaining to her: that is
I cannot. That *He* cannot desist from path, from choice.
His, His. That *He* loves her but cannot walk away from
that: *His* work. She paralyzes him. That perhaps *He*,
         well ... *He* does not love her.

The *He*'s surveyed. The *He*'s investigated. Time and
again they come to check him out. *He* continues. *He*
finds seniors who understand him, who wish, in the
beginning at least and last, to help him: to publish him.
He debases himself before them: "The Greats depress me
and exalt me by turn" / "*Schlägt mich nieder und erhebt
mich wechselsweise.*" *His* letters to them grovel. *He* is
speaking to gods but gods do never answer -- at any rate
in language that *He* can understand. This not a time for
poets. "This not a place for the work of poets" / "*nicht
      empfänglich für die Gesänge der Dichterkunst.*"

Perhaps this never will be. How can our poets work in this
no time, no space, no listening, no understanding? Here too:
I am/I am not. Studenthood was not too painful. Results were
granted. Feathers placed in my hair, my hat. Badges pinned
on my breast: papers attesting to the passage of that time.
Even submitted, for my final paper, a sheaf of poems: Ho?
And the taught eventually taught. It was impossible to find
anything less to live on. And *He* was teaching younger kids;
trying to bring them into the realm of reason, philosophy if
need be. *I am/I am not.* It is a hideous waiting period before
ambition -- before that desperate attempt to clothe the self
into some fair achievement: something the world would pay
attention to, read, publish, send out to multitudes of lands,

countries, a world is made of around bright shores of ocean,
encompass the wide world in short -- no single boundary.
Gods would now look down to him at last, smiling, smiling:
Yes, you made it. Came, Conquered. You are the sins of the
almighty gods.

And *He* writes out the story. *He* accumulates those stories that
go into the story -- because, because, there is but just one story.
He waits for her. *He* practices with "hers." With plural "her."
He is dissatisfied: *He* will not stay with them; *He* will not keep
them; *He* will not take them to *His* heart. They sadden at the
loss of such a person. *He* who was said "to walk Apollo-like
through space" / "*als schritte Apollo durch den Saal*," rooms,
gardens: *He* who seemed to walk and breathe in Hall just like
a god of poetry. And still the Greats went certain to uncertain:
looked down on him: holding their smiles in check. Keeping
them tight. Preserving them. *Aber I* am / *Aber I* am not. *I* own
no single language.

For the day when *He* would spring forth and the sky turned to
abundance of all Blues, Blue which would never fade. Blue
which no cloud effaced. Blue of *His* mighty rivers. Blue of *His*
blood running in those veins *He* thought *He* might cut into -- Oh,
one day, perhaps with hers. Together in full time would break,
would in the end break down the solitude, that loss, that: Never
will we see our life again. And if the Blue did not arrive, did not
materialize. *Jetzt*. Did not now sacrifice *His* throat under the altar.

Here was *His* cosmos out of *Theogony*. First after Chaos
came the full-breasted Gaia: our Earth to be the everlasting
basis for all beings. And she creates Ouranos: Sky of stars.
Born of the Sky and Earth (incest a'plenty) comes next: the
Okeanos: that Deep Sea, also the Titans. One of the Giants,
the Hyperion, father of light, Helios Immortal Sun; shining
Selene Moon; our nightly treasure, Mnemosyne, mother of
the Nine Muses and the last born, most dire, most horrible:
Kronos (all latter born) World Time: father of Zeus. Then
from Empedokles of Agrigentum, Sicily, *He* takes a physics:
Earth, Air, Water, Fire - composing now, or decomposing
now at the behest of Love or Strife: *hen diapheron eautō*.
Much else in there including Demeter: the Corn, Mother of
My Persephone ... But if you do not favor this reading of the
lists keep trying for yourselves: who once had sex with whom
and who bore which divinity - for few agree on Hesiod's, his
sparagmatic charts. Meanwhile you need to recognize that
such a poetry must be initiatic - music as much as literature:
     and this may be the only music that *I* speak.

And, therefore how to know which divine name came down
to him from ancient times? Was it the crazy god of wine, that
Dionysus, who brought a smile into the primal mind, primal
philosopher -- Plato, his Socrates -- or was it then a cosmic
Son, descending into death for to bring back the dead: a Prince
of Peace? Poets bring peace if they are heard and not vast loads
of doubtful myth raised by human desire for aid & sustenance.
He fought throughout his life to bring the gods of Hellas into
the folds of his own country. But bound to name the gods of that
"own country" so that the folk could recognize his meaning and
be comforted. And doubt was *His* from birth to end as well as
certainty over the poet's task: to certify that man and nature are of
one blood and brain, the one/the all but of a single substance for,
without this, the race would perish in its ignorance: "*Es ist der
Abend der Zeit*" / "It is the end of time" will come to pass. We

name a coming. We certify it. The coming end of Green is obvious in all our acts. All other witnessing is absolutely lost, is absolutely pointless.

I's childhood. Family parked: summer & winter holydays in a
land of original freedom. Fragrant meadows, encircling high Alps,
hurrying mountain streams to climb up rock by rock: flower by
flower identified, tanned cow licking a pair of hands held in the
back while leaning on a fence: the shock of it! The liquid warmth!
He too, considering that land as Fatherland of Liberty, kin in the
heart to his own *Vaterland,* his Swabia, gone there in early youth.

I am/I am not. Here in a quietness will never cease. Am in a quiet
I cannot hear. *He* is as quiet on the day of days. *His* eyes descend
on her. It is a preparation. *She* is the earth-the sky-the underworld.
There is no looking back. But has not seen her yet. Met simulacra
there perhaps, may have enjoyed one, two or three but not in those
vast meadows, not on those slopes like cataracts of sunshine blazing
down mountain sides. Thinking of revolution too, thinking it might

arrive (on peoples' knees to ground in slavery) No! in a burst of light
to *His* own country may freedom shine at last, that folks move free in
every walk of life! But revolution breaks to tragedy, heads roll, a pain
atrocious chokes the interminable parable of Freedom. Freedom will
never come, armies will now be formed, will overrun the fatherlands
of poets. Murder enthroned again. Seeming the land of Freedom: in
that a home from home was not. Quiet now. Quiet not. Canton Vaud:

The aged owners rough proto-nazis: their thoughts on the new power
rising further north. An Asian kid, larger than other kids, holding *My*
arm behind *My* back - no gentle cowlick. "Now *heil* to that dictator ...
or risk a broken limb!" And if not broken severely hurt. Taken
nightly to pray in corridors. Punished for wetting beds. Children put
out on deck chairs postprandially examining each other's parts under
the blankets, learning the alphabet of life. Thus "sex."

Oh! flying over snow. Oh! *I*: the single sport beloved and years after
the most substantial war, found far too tall to take that up again -- so
nose falls into snow. Again. Again. *He*: shame of it! The terminus of
sport! Thinks of the sullen Halls back at the college; tedious homework,

tedious determinisms; single goal exercises, blight of the age-old fears; dying misunderstandings; worships no single soul wishes to undertake -- while these, these holy ones, swearing passionate love for ages down the line, seared whole by poetry and by philosophy - this is return back into intolerable adumbration, no road to follow; and no desire ever fulfilled.

He is a failure. *I* am a failure. Will be ever a failure.

Later, rush through a field mantled in snow, snow pouring down, last call, last laugh for Primavera -- will the legs last? *I* fall to crevices in one great field, soon capable of feeding hundreds of animals and there, behind a sun, more snow descending, more wet grass underfoot: *I* see the sport end soon: hot drinks, ham sandwiches, perhaps a pickle, cakes of the Land of Liberty's earliest trials. But these are memories? Or shades of memories, minute selections? Minute particulars from pasts but barely lived through since and now forgotten in all their burning details. Now desert sands smother any forgotten snow, forgotten sports. If there's an end to dying not one can tell of it. Not one *dixit* perhaps.

A poem has a date - but whatever the date, it has to gather into a presence. There has to be an opening, an "open" that allows what must appear into its own appearance. So say, with reason, some of today's philosophers. There may occur a sense that there's a start, there's a beginning, that such a start will lead direction, that the direction will improve any experience, that it will be a favorable direction. Whatever sadness then prevailing, a sadness due to an own world emptying, the movement into that direction will sure improve this present over past. This is the usual accepted present in our culture. The poem then travels into and ends in affirmation. Say: Is it possible for poems not to end in affirmation? Can poetry, by its own very nature as something which is aperture to lifetime, to a life moment and, in its own happiest movement, reaches to its own end -- not end in "Yes"? However much of "sad" now is inside a poem, can the full work end in a "No" rather than in acceptance?

But if, however, there were a ground of sadness, a ground so deep, lying below the ice of hell if need be (diagnosis), a pavement under which no single bone from any previous culture could be found, so that the fair remembrance of a good not only would deliver no such respite but lead only to louder, interminable sobs, spreading spoiled color over every thing, person, or situation that could be counted or imagined so that there never would be any change: an inability at altering, oh! but a single drop of water turning to wine would never bring a penitent back to a one and only home. All caves shut down, an infernal spoil of trying to reach down into a nether depth far too unfeasible. No: there could not be up. Nor could be down: but only the one weather and its immortal stars unchanging, stars seeming petrified by looking down at grief unchangeable. Depth. Depression. Single, Unalterable Mood. Full Tedium Vitae thrown at the teeth of a foul century. No single balm, no medication leading into good; and no improvement or cessation. And yet even a poem *now*, by dint of being poem *here*, ends in a "Yes." We say Amen.

The roses never looked so good before we gained a dormant garden
help. But roses burn in just one day of this appalling desert heat. An
effervescent sun burning the roses as *I* must wish it would inflame all
features of the abhorrent politicians plunging a nation into ruin ...
         and archaeology! We look in vain for faces from a human past.

Merely to glimpse those faces - and they are fed to us each day dumb
media write of the disgusting swine - leads into sickness of the spirit,
even to suicide of the eternal mind. *I am* / *I am not*. Unhappy daily at
a one we once called "life" now in a constant downgrade into the latest
updated slavery. "*Einst*" / "At one time." So there were not, for this one
("this one" is *I*), shades of the prison house that had "begun" to close:
they'd been so definitely closed by the king spider's window. Yet *He*,
the not yet famed and celebrated one, threw up on a lost childhood to
gather spirit from love & claims. "*Jetzt*" / "At this time": ambition: a
most primal devil held to heart: in such pursuit an endless sadness since
                  fame could not be guaranteed.

Oh, we are seeming free! We live democracy. We not: NO - not divided
into small principalities at the hard mercy of autocratic princes. We harbor
imbecilic faith groups who spend their hymns destroying minds -- but we're
not at lifelong mercy of consistoria governing lives as *His* was governed
until death. The best of us have known the radical philosopher: the Kant
from Königsberg: his skepticism laid mines under that faith. At the start,
in the beginning: wholeness, a vast infinity. When shades had gathered:
breaks, classes, poverty. But thus could enter world -- and opposition
would manifest as battle with the world, tension forever and everlasting
motion. Likewise the art of poetry, in nature infinite, demands form's
limitations to speak at all. A ceaseless mode of discontent is daily bread
and wine: the inability to be pure spirit in the world's grip measures the
endless slavery. But yet there are surprises: "If what you bear inside you as
truth ever approaches you as beauty" / "*Wenn Dir als Schönheit entgegen-
kommt*" -- accept it gratefully for you need every helpful hand Nature
                  can offer you.

Where do *I* turn? Which country have not been to? Which disappointment still to be wept at? The world, a cyclopaedia of gorgeous places now known by all and overrun by all. All populations swell, all sights to fill the heart to overflowing: trashed. Disaster strikes: no mention of the fact that more will follow in its wake: that, finally, the planet loses its battle with mankind in the umpteenth extinction. Did *He* divine this? *His* tears for beauty's sake manifest urgent purpose and they suggest it.

This land is oil's; this land is gas's; this land is minerals';
this land is metals'; this land is electricity's; this land is
propane's; this land is bones'; this land is jewels'. This land
is burning's; this land is digging's; this land is mining's; this
land is excavating's; this land is quarrying's; dredging's;
drilling's; tunneling's; fracking's. This land is bombing's;
gassing's; this land is subject to nuclearization. This land is
open to subtraction; redistricting; all mortgaging; theft; tax;
development. This land is open to devaluation; to alienation;
to all abstractions; to all disfigurations. This land is open to
uglifications; to flood, to arson; to destruction: in one form
or another it can be taken from you -- although in truth you
never owned it in the first place: but by misunderstanding.

However many pages were signed over; how many affidavits
were designed to certify an ownership; how many bona fide
lawyers, estate agents, bankers, accountants were drawn into
proceedings to swear the land is owned by he who sits on it,
no one under this crest, this emblem, shield or flag can ever
claim to be a lord or lady over it. For centuries the people of
this land claimed it was motherland or fatherland; for years
they fought some other lands for it; for days they marched
over the land with noise and shouting. The land in truth was
never theirs; they never came into their own; there was no
ownership involved -- for everything initially had borne
another mark than theirs. No growth into a patrimony, or
matrimony, or any grant that they could recognize. And
was no coming into their own nation. And notwithstanding
all men of war; all the campaigns and all the revolutions,
the day would never dawn over their heads; nightfall would
never fade over their houses. Deep down under the earth,
the inadmissible abyss would yield no treasure. High up
the sky's ecstatic light would never yield the sight of stars,
of the deep Aether in which the angels walked, in which
the gods prepared their love to float above their worshipers
to bring them any certainty some space of life were theirs.

I have been walking ground throughout this world, each
time enslaved to some deep country in the spirit that *I*
would recognize, make my own, call my own. This right
should by some law be every human's. Each time *I* landed
from the sea, or rode whatever vehicle over the land, arriving
to some promising adventure, a first and foremost love would
bend into some work; the *lares & penates* would be greeted
at some house gate; acceptable companions be discovered
to sign community. That is what my progenitor had looked for
all *His* life, fallen in love with all *His* life -- until the others'
unrecognizable behavior had frightened him, strengthened
His desire to call back solitude. *I* sense that solitude as well
and know there is no greater strength than in acceptance -
yet, back there, you could find community, you could find
brotherhood and sisterhood; you could find love. Ah! what a
word is "love;" how sole it is; how unaffordable it stays deep
in the mind! It stays deep Selah! *I* am a citizen of everything
and nothing. *I* live in everywhere and nowhere. *I* sleep in
silences, sing in absences, never bring home a daily bread
untainted. *I* am quietly "mad" though not incarcerated. To
                    be quietly "mad." You grant me that.

In the far distance *I* see roses. In the far distance *I* can smell
lilac. There is the place where all the flowers bloom: the ones
I did not find in this terrain. *I* know that there are people there.
They cannot see me. They do not know me. They never will.
Our man, our holy poet knew that some distant day a present
darkness would abstain from people and a so distant and so
forgotten glory in the past would be recovered: it was a plot
to found a *Patria*. Now it is not available. A hell mistook for
progress grew uncontrollably throughout this epoch. A future
now became a lasting situation and *He* disguised himself to it
                    without regret.

The oscillation! Between being a no one, cold, apathetic,
deadly and then a sudden spring-jet of ecstatic joy: a fate
of moments. Here too, the passage of the pessimist into
his basis as an optimist quick as the flowing mercury: a
happenstance. The cold, interminable heavy wish to die
lightened by but a moment's sudden comfort, returns to
suicidal rage in but a flash. Our man alas is cyclothymic.
Perhaps it is the sense that aged humans -- (the bird, the
animal, not so: surely they die in an unearthly quiet minus
a thought granted to nothingness) -- both are alive & dead
at the same time; continue work and give up work in the
same sheer discomfort, a sense acute at every moment of
the day - too carried into sleep when all the bedclothes
suddenly fall moved by unwitnessed thrashings of a corpse
to be, from off the bed and onto ground. *I am/I am not ...*
I am alive/*I* die.

Oh, then there is the placement of these miseries. One time,
the place *He* lives in seems like death, obscenity the case
among its people, the business people most especially - then,
for *Her* sake, who lives there utterly beyond *Her* space & time,
in exile from *Her* proper ages -- the place is, ah! the navel of
the world -- thus harking back to Delphi of the Greeks, *His*
chosen people. And yet the mistress to the sage of Weimar
sees in this amorous encounter without any action, something
as "*etwas Wertherisches*" / "as Werther-like": call it a doom
in waiting. *I* too have loved & hated in one breath. Think
now of here, these zoomorphic deserts totally occupied by
devastating beasts: killers of gardens; cars; home-built tools;
machines (desert defined by those public-relations imbeciles
as "true" when "false" is just as open to their calculations).
Here *I*'ve seen clouds depend from Paradise, cut by the gods
into their own desires: no shapes like these were ever seen in
other skyscapes by human eyes, geometry devised by human
mind, no unachievable designs painted by human hand: there
in the gods' country high above earth, bathed in the utmost

altitude of sky! Down too, as in a mirror's game since gods
live everywhere, the deepest oceanic pit below the earth, this
pit dug thru the planet's uttermost limits defines the splendid
country of my heart!

A nation bred, as ever nation was, in violence, people addicted,
like angry prophets, to a cult of guns, cannot breed speakers who
speak with open voice, bluntly in criticizing this or that disaster
among those who believe this is "democracy." *Hombre* = 1 vote:
this signifies? This changes by one jot the fate of nations? While
things below the animal drive ruling houses, while ruling classes
obscenely rich descend way down in thought, speech, action,
collapse below the animals? All things commented on go *sotto
voce* from one ear to another -- never in public space. This way
a nation can begin to die, (this way my love, my lovely nation),
this way a nation can destroy itself, this way a nation murders
many peoples, under the guiding chiefs, the absences-of-mind,
blathering day to night in endlessly repeated communication
systems like bloated vermin: while citizens presented with huge
begging bowls are meant to pay for services the governors should
govern: Good fortune to us poets since no one ever listens: "*Wir
leben in dem Dichterklima nicht*" / "This is no climate for us the
poets": Go swallow that!

Always there is a hope of peace, the peace achieved, the
peace in doubt, the peace desired, a peace Oh! longed for,
a yearning for a peace: the fear that peace will never come,
a sense that peace is now desire and cannot be achievement.
Summon a gathering to celebrate this peace, Oh most elusive
of all desires! Now set the togetherness on top of a great alp.

Sky's Master Sun shines on that mountain top between the
celebrators. The Lord of Peace enthroned within that Sun
receives the celebrators one by one: they carrying names
of all the gods that have been known before, all the gods
present, all gods to come -- since there's a plethora of gods,
as many as the substances of earth require to flourish. This
is the evening of our time. New mediations flocking home.
Then comes a leading god, born out of wedlock: Son of &
to the Lord of Peace. This younger god stands in a flesh as
Son presented to a Father, the King of Peace. This younger
Son is Prince of Peace. The King undresses younger Prince
leaving him naked. The Prince gathers his limbs into a giant
body - a form far greater than he stood in before. The King
lays him on middle earth between the celebrators' seatings.
Then he divides the arms of the huge Prince and nails them
pointing outward as a tree's main branches, securing thus his
Prince as motionless. The Prince's body dissolves in earth,
he is the fruitfulness of earth. He drinks from the roaring Sun
above him and then transforms into the planet men see from
Earth: the Sun feeding mankind. The celebrators then send
flights of help with cups in which to catch his blood: and that
they drink in full --- mouthfuls of earth from hilltop serving
to wash down a communal blood. Thus temples are assembled.

When our compatriots came down the Danube into the Black
Sea we and the races there (known as the Children of the Sun)
contracted marriages and, out of these, "the finest and most
beautiful in all of humankind were born:" / "*Schöner, denn
Alles, // Was vor und nach / von Menschen sich nannt', ein*

Geschlecht auf." / "How mythic ideologies threaten these
        present diverse generations!"

The Sun on earth arises out of Asia and marches West, arriving
at the very gates of landscapes men recognize as home. Waters
of all the rivers known to them rush from the Western highlands
back toward East, a gift of the home counties. Now: have *you*
ever been out to those Easts? Beyond the Athens & the Spartas
(you have not even seen those -- only imagined them at will)
have you a knowledge of Asian treasures? Let me come in as
soul, as "anima," and take you, Dear One, to the farthest Easts
this planet worships. Take you to Isfahan of blinding light --
white cover for its sapphire mosques; on out to India: its soul
Ajanta of the divinest paintings; out to the Taj, the burial of
heaven's wives; out into Khajuraho; a celebration of the body's
love. Then on into Angkor of deep Cambodias; Pagan of the
deep Burmas; Borobadur of the deep Indonesias. And over to
the Dunhuang's caves in deepest China; the celebrated gardens
of a rash Japan: all these "and more" as people urge right now,
tempting interminably the populace to spend again-again as if
this century knew nothing beyond their spending: building for
an uncertain, virtually fatal future being the only end they might
wish to ignore. How fortunate you were, dear friend, to know
so little of the earth beyond your property so that the property
would never need to be enlarged, or bettered in its decorations,
or in its accesses - as everything now in this century requires to
be "improved." And thus destroyed by over-population and the
desire for more, forever more, as the earth shrinks beneath them,
as Sun rises again into the skies to work annihilation on the earth.

Now this the breaking of a master love. *Love can be / Love can be not.* Love can be broken by the gods. By fire or water, parents, friends, children, the vagaries of gender. Just name the enemy: you're home. This *I*, in a green night of Europe, one night out of a thousand nights of hope and young desire, in never fading recollection. Lie helplessly beside the perfect body while it will not respond, it will not move, it will not help, it won't, it won't reciprocate and the whole night, alas, goes by destroyed for ever. The subject of a search, of an experiment in sexuality, a girl's experiment that later broke the hopes of many boys. Decades long gone: never forgotten. One time potential bride who would not change her "faith" because *I's* father made a condition of it, or did not wish for a new "faith." The marriage cancelled. Then came one wife, beloved in good time, mother of children, lifelong dearest friend. Then came another -- utter working companionship, also a life-enhancing friend.

He writes: "*es giebt ein Wesen aus der Welt:*" / "there is a being on this earth: the Athenäa" / "*die Athenerin,*" this did I call her first before I named her just Diotima. O! clear, that beautiful complexion out of Titian and, as I asked another friend, "*Nicht wahr, eine Griechin?*" / "A Greek -- now isn't *She?*" As for Diotima in Plato: a Greek philosopher. (And it was said that I, this Hölder, strange! was glad to physically resemble D.'s very brother!) "*She* is in exile from her proper times! Truth it's impossible to think of earthly things when *She* is present -- which is why desperately little can be said of her. I have moved out of suffering, of the invisible despair that ate away my life, my work, my very being as a poet; I am in a new world." Then, as for *I*, back in my youth's own time it is this father, this businessman, this man of finance, yanking the "*I*," a kid, even when middle-aged, into his lair, forbidding him to live the life of poetry or making it so hard, so difficult, another life had to be added on to the basic life thus weakening that life for many years.

Thus it was fated: *He* had to work below her station, thrown
to her company by his too close position: the education of
her children. Was *He* an equal in the house -- at parties, teas,
dinners, conversations, picnics and trips abroad: or was *He*
but a slightly better servant to be dispensed with when serious
togethers were involved? One such O! so much wanted, loved,
so much desired, passing close-up, or reading her some work,
must have tipped up the scale of his demeanors and *He* was
out! And after that: the fevered letters, the once a week walks
by her house hoping that they could see each other until, at last,
the spell had to be broken, he had to leave her neighborhood …
"*Geh unter, schöne Sonne, sie achteten Nur wenigh Dein*" / "Go
down, you lovely Sun, they paid you scant attention" - or say
"*Aber die Sonne des Geists, die schönerer Welt ist hinunter?*" /
"But then the Sun of spirit, the loveliest of worlds has set once
and for all?"

And whether soon, or whether late, the person-life must be
lodging below the poet-life and hope must be abandoned in
order to become - not only poetry - but no thing else on earth
that can be thought of. What are they then to you O Song!
Pure Song? those other hopes, those other works? It's true that
I shall die but as for you: you move another way. And now *He*
works as if the climate *were* permission for the work, as if his
youth commissioned him to fame, as if those difficult, hard,
painful masters could not make him feel so small! so small!
and could go back into their dens when *He* had called so loud
to them for sustenance. Shame on their silence when *He* asked
for help and, weary or disgruntled with his pleas, not certain *He*
was in for real, for Germany, they caused him to go back upon
his plans! *He* had to ask for money yet again from a tough Ma:
a man of thirty-some -- thus merely asking for his patrimony!
He had to worry that one would help Diotima "*um nicht enlich
zu vertrauern*" / "so that her sadness should not be the end of
her." For him: "*ich hätte manchmal die Seele mir ausweinen
müssen, wenn ich es aussprechen wollte.*" / "If I had tried to say
my whole misery, I think I should have wept the soul out of my
body -- and been way gone from hence." She wrote: "Our love

cannot be taken from us." *She* wrote: "But our unseen, invisible belongings to each other will last, perdure, and will continue, while life … This life is short."

The oracles declare, each, every single one, throughout
the land: the land has been estranged: intolerable sin has
been committed. The sin performed under a Tree of Life.
And the *Erde Vater* the Zeus, the *Schlachtgeist* the Ares,
the *Geist der Liebe* Eros and the *Friedensgeist,* Lord of our
Peace, then *Hades,* Head of each single Underworld -- *all*
have declared the race of man must be extinguished if that
one sinner not be banished. The sinner now drives himself
mad with queries as to whom, or what, has spoiled the land
for *He* sees in himself no evil act such as the law has called it.
Or sees not yet - although transgendered ancient lords have
pierced it. Questions himself over and over, day and night,
for *He* has quite forgotten that, to gain *His* pleasure, *He* has
endangered, and even massacred, *His* own forefathers. The
He, the broken heart of the translator, together with the sinner,
obsesses about learning, studying, examining, disclosing and
then interpreting *His* broken life. The revelation and the end
of time occur together. *He* passes from the mother-lover -- *He*
who had never found a common ground with mother --- to a
single daughter and there *He* stays, in roofless admiration. *She*
is the fruit of all his work, end of successes, his long eternity.

She is the only love, only true love, of a whole life's beginning,
also end. And *She*'s condemned to death because *She* has stood
up to every tyranny *She* knew the secret of. So see you, men
and women of my land, going the final length of my sweet life
and witnessing, since you must bring me down, the Sun's last
light. Never again? Never again? To see the gardens of this life
wake in the morning, color this earth with golden light? Never
again? The god of death, the *Hades* of existence, who watches
us at every step, at every turning in our lives, waiting to swallow
us in his dark kingdom: he takes me down to the one final river
we all traverse to make an end of it. And I cannot be married for
now already married, cannot be married to my poet's song; I
cannot hear his song, his song of praise, a wedding song, for I
am married to a river. I have been laid to waste, this body bent

and crouched, shrunk, sent to the other side, the no return, the
side of sleep, chained to the ivy and slow stones, washing my
throat with tears of snow and ice. Gone, gone again to more, to
furthermore and stars.

Hades searching the world for the far shores of Hindustan
to bring back all ancestral wildness of the Eastern blood, to set
back Asia into beloved Greece - so that its peoples might be
helped to bring the wildness to clarity. Wild Hellas turning
into clarity. And then the morning springtime light of clarity
Hellas's peoples knew in their minds, knew in their bones,
washing into their own. O! paradisal hands to make beauty
never seen once before and hardly ever seen again or since.
He wished to bring it to our shores, into our sullen thoughts.
Sober and dull we were, so massively in need of passion.
And the new world which came out of the old: more sober
and more dull continues to require that classic clarity. If it
will not obliterate its mental chains, letting them fall into
the deathless ocean, the newness of this world will soon
evaporate and man will have to wait such further centuries
as his own crass stupidity might generate. Or not: a question.

The Case, in this case, of a younger sibling in love with
painting. It's *I*, okay? gathers the family with a proposal:
Let just what can be spared out of the patrimony be given
to the sibling now instead of at the death of parents -- and
let the sibling go to find himself a cottage in the country
and do his painting. For some *in toto* unaccountable, dumb
decision of a sense of duty, sibling refuses and ruins his
life. Just so, but in some different tones, this *I* continues
into scholarship when he would far prefer to live for poetry.

Der Abschied / The Farewell. The *He*, after departing love,
(they have decided to spare it from cold delinquency)
settles away from her and gives his all to poetry & art,
the single things he cares for. Sorrow is battled. Despair
is battled. Depression battled. Hopelessness battled too.
"*So weiß ich, was ich gewollt habe.*" / "And even if my
inner life never achieves a clear, abundant language,
        at least I'll be aware of what I have desired."

Mother still holds the purse. But in *His* knowledge, an
ever-growing knowledge of what *He* really is, *He* finally
points out to her how noxious is her power above his head,
declares his state and claims that, if *He* fails, *He* will do as
she wishes and take the humblest job as pastor that can be
found or even an assistanceship in quiet, rural space. *He*
clarifies his sense that *He* has never known his mother's
love, or her esteem: *"daß Sie keine Freude an mir hätten."*

And, as for politics, *He* wishes for the French to conquer
and bring "Republic" into German parlance. Just so, the "*I*"
awaits a time when language can at last be spoken as it is
meant to be and all the soft "liberal" tones the nation won't
abandon even in this great crisis of history can be drowned
out. The truth of it: *I* cannot stand the stench. Time for a
quintessential number of necessary things to be performed

by government and not by charities endlessly waving their depthless begging bowls under our noses. The poor to be unpoored. The homeless to be homed. Hurt migrants to be accommodated in their own countries with our miraculously overgrown and overpowering *Gelt*. The sick to get whatever care they need for free in any doctor's office, or any hospital. All the disabled likewise. Death penalty abolished. Police abuse abolished. Imbecile cult of guns and murder ended. The mass incarceration on a financial basis to be abolished. Race, Gender questions totally squared once and for all. The mega-rich to be compelled to give until they bleed (without losing their homes).

The Land to be preserved in health and all its Creatures. The Climate to be governed by our reason, not by our greed. All the desiderata without one exception to be enacted in plain cold language without incompetence, corruption, ignorance, prejudice. The excremental slime of potential dictators to be invalidated: face up the present need to do without civility. All matter of importance to the polity be solved by wise researchers, scholars in every single field the Nation's life must rest upon and be insured. Needless to say, a thousand other issues need to be looked at and resolved. Needs to be recognized, needs to be understood (knife in the head) that this is still, amongst all other things, a seemingly incurable racist inferno totally blind to that which it can't recognize in crime, in massacre: the lynching capital of world. Readers accustomed to civility will qualify this stanza as a rant. It is but ceasing: we must desist from language games and other puerilities. It is but honesty.

"Die Welt hat meinen Geist von früher Jugend an in sich zurükgescheucht, und daran leid' ich noch immer ... ich scheue das Gemeine und Gewöhnliche im wirklichen Leben zu sehr" / "The world drove my spirit back into itself even in childhood and I am still in danger from that suppression ... I am too timid for what is coarse and so banal in every day's existence." Adding: "I must make use of what is so destructive and draw up some advantage from that loss ..."

The most mysterious moment, far more mysterious than any birth in nature. A word, a run of words, moves from the poet's mind (throat, nostrils, mouth) onto a page. Poet dictates. And poet, in that vast immediacy, shares with potential readers - perhaps you? - out of so many maybe readers of the poem. Poet says "Calling! This poem calls you. Are you available? Do you accept a call?" In the face of time. The poet serves with all the other poets a major potlatch in the teeth of time. The guests arrive into this tragic era bereft of their ancient gods. This time sick with the satanic sickness of our nihilism. And so the call has to go out, forth from the dawn, to reach the present time, to greet the present gods: "*gegenwärtige Götter.*" The gods of now are not the ancient gods. They are the longed-for visitors of now. And not extinguished as night pretends they are: simply they have departed, gone far away. Or else *I* must pretend that they are far away. Only before the dawn, the morning light, before heavenly light descends on earth, *I* must name them inside my peace. And standing *here*, *I* am the poet of my poem.

The far away? But if they are so close, does close mean *almost* close or else *too* close? "*Nah ist und schwer zu fassen der Gott.*" / "Near is and yet hard to take hold of is the God." Hard at the poet's face, the news takes seemingly endless time and, so, the coming is the more painful and more difficult. And hard acceptance of the gift the gods are offering, the gift of speech, of poem. Pressed by a harsh necessity, a need that can perhaps be seen as sacred, being the basis of a life without the which a life does not exist. Obscure and hidden in deep cloud, the name must be -- god name / gods' names -- spoken in silence. Naming, knowing of naming, ends by a call from those approaching. Veiled those who come, approach -- and *I* must name them. And if the veiled emerge out of the sacred, *I* must be silent. But if silence

prevails then that which must be stated has to be that
highest knowledge possible and this has to be given
over to all other men. Not held alone inside the poet's
mind. Thus the gods named by me in inmost peace. And
this is way before the morning of the gods, when fire
covers the sky. The god caparisoned in steel appears.
Beaten steel sparks.

Soil faints away. Its absence can be called "abyss." Long
and heavy is the approaching word. The servants of the
sky move forward to the named abyss searching for holy
peace. And those, the present gods who can feel nothing
by themselves and have no sense of being, and neither
sense of death - who in a way have no existence but in
the minds of humans who can know them, name them,
worship them - gods who must need others to feel for
them, with conscience of existing and thus of being
mortal, that dreaded knowledge. Gods the compassion
carriers without any incendiary abyss of feeling. Just
below them, the demigods or Heroes, who can help
men: the Dionysus, the Heracles, the Christ. As well
as the great rivers ever loved. The poet is that other
whom the gods require. The gods have need. The poet
answers and provides. This is the legend of the sky's
echo. *He* names them so that the poet owns *His* own
sovereign role, that part *He* acts on earth. And when
celestial light descends, *He* willingly holds in *His* head
past light and lips withholding poem. Withholds until
He writes and writing's done.

And so the fiction enters - because the history does not.
The letters written beyond the meeting, when parting was
the only source to come. No matter all her Come! & Come!
again / But do not come! it is too dangerous! - yet how can
this all-whole be split in all these ways, be so discolored,
so dishonored? We'll never know how *She* lay down and
died -- too soon. How mind, his own *He* claimed, moved
toward dissolution or to piecemeal politeness toward the
mother spirit who had killed him. As for the *I* re love, *She*
who adored the *I,* a son, and yet could not protect him
from the father, from all the fathers in the business world
(read scholars' world). Whose only letter to the father we
now possess together with a hundred letters *He* tried to be
forgiven by, while fighting all the time for clarity. Clarity!

He'd wanted infinite. *He*'d wanted absolute. The purity of
the deep ocean islands back in the mother world where the
sufficient and the lacking, the prodigal, the penury gave
rise together to the Son of love. The Sun of love and, Lord,
bring in the Moon before it is too late! There *He* had said
a thousand and one farewells, there had attempted to avoid
all passion except the race toward the enemy, a crushing of
the enemy to bring to birth a novel world. The whole thrust
Hyperactive. And if it took for him the love of men for men,
the handing of a girl into the hands of other men, that too
would prove part of the sum of love without a threat to love.
Wanted Perfection. Wholeness. Completion's in the cards.
Yet never could *He* bring desire and satisfaction to the brink
of consummation. Ever the split: presence and absence were
so far linked together, his eye could not bear with the other
eye in a summation.

Do this / Do that. No, do not do a thing. Quick pass the time.
Quickly pass over this, pass over that. No, do not pass. Live
here, live there, give up the scribing, give up the scripture,
burn out whole libraries of text. Copy them all before the fire,

republish them. Throw letters from a window, hide letters in a hedge, position self behind her hedge just so it can be seen from the window upstairs. If the curtains closed *She* will not come down, if they are open -- will. *He* visits every time -- be they his visits once a week, or once every six weeks, or many months can pass if visitors arrive, gobble up the time. And all the while, hands ache to touch; lips ache to comprehend the total sum of love, the sprouts of adoration. Distant grows hope, grows possibility, more and more savage the murmured wisps, the murmurations of the town: oh, yes, *She* must think this, *She* must think that, and doubtless *She* must do both this and that. Leaving aside what *He* can do, just walking past her hedges. Paper covered in tears. Writer sliding into the signatures of tears, thus sometimes near unreadable. Returning into home, *He* coming back to home so that there is no notice, so that the broken tongues of love and admiration can remain on course, so that suspicion dies with every word, every false word, all false description, all subterfuges break with the dying day on this return. Until the next one. A next one after that. Until O! God! discovery, at first so sad, cracks our tragic acceptances, confirms a criminality of move into and out of love's demise.

From *"Menons klagen um Diotima"* / "Menon's
     Lament for Diotima"

***

*"Celebrate, yes – but what? I'd gladly sing with
others since now alone anything godly won't
ring true. This is, I know, ill-doing on my part,
my sinews maimed: only because of this I flag
from the very start and stay numb all day long,
a child moping and dumb. At times a cold tear
clouds my eyes and the field's flowers, bird
song: these heraldries of heaven bearers of joy
bring on in me sheer sadness: in my cold heart
soul-giving suns dawn iced, infertile, feeble as
rays of night. Oh! thus futile & empty -- walls
of a prison heaven presses down on me a load,
smothering load of pain over my lowered head."*

***

*"But you who even then, already at the crossroads,
when I fell at your feet, showed me the way to
comfort, taught me to see the greatness, to sing
with more of gentle beauty, joy more serene --
the gods (silent as gods yourself: you god-child)
will you appear to me? Greet me once more,
raising me up into your quiet, tell me again of
things we know? Look here, in front of you, I
weep and cry, although remembering the better
times now past, deep in my soul I feel terrible
shame. For such a long, long time, weary over
the earth, still am accustomed to you – seek
you in wilds, Spirit of me. But all for nothing:
whole years have now gone by since you and I
we walked in evening late, bathed in an evil glow."*

*"You only you, light of your own, O heroine, stay
still inside the light, your patience keeping you
loving and kind, and you're not lonely: enough
playmates around where in the rose beds you
are blooming and resting with the flowers of a
year. And the Father himself, through the balm-
inhaling Muses, sends you those warm, southerly
cradle-songs. Yes, She is quite the same! From
head to heels She's still the Athenäa, quiet and
poised as ever, She hovers in my eyes. And as
a blessing your radiance falls over all mortals,
you tender soul, down from your brow wrapt
in deep thought, yet still serene, you prove to me,
tell me that I may pass it on to all who doubt as
I doubt: that care and anger pale at enduring
joy -- and that the day still shines a golden end."*

***

*"Once more then I'll thank you up in heaven and
now, once more, my prayer can rise up from a
heart unoppressed. And as before when I stood
with her on a sun-lavished hill, a god now speaks
to me inside a temple. So, I will live then! Fresh
spring, fresh green! As from a hallowed lyre, on
down from silvered peaks, Apollo's mountains now
sing out. Come; it was like a dream: wings' wounds
have healed, brought back to youth all your old
hopes alive. And recognizing greatness is that much,
yet much remains yet to be done and one who loved
as you loved can only join the gods. You lead us then,
you solemn ones, hours of Communion, youthful ones,
stay with us, holy forward looks, and pious prayers,
and you our Inspirations, and all you kindly spirits
who like to look after lovers, be with them where
they live. Stay with us two until, upon communal*

ground, now reunited: where when they're due to
come, all blessed souls return. Where the eagles are,
the planets too, the Father's heralds and the Muses
still, where lovers started, there we shall meet again,
or here on a dew-covered island where what is ours
for once, blooms that a garden marries, all our poems
ring true, springs stay lovely much longer and yet
another year, a new year of our souls can resurrect."

For him the rivers carried life backward and forward. *He* loved them dearly as the demigods, brothers and sisters to other demigods: the poets. True that the rivers begin high in some deserted alps or towering mountains and true that they work downward as they move toward sea. But in the poetry, you cannot ever trust, cannot ever be sure, a stream for him also does not carry back whatever loads it met on the sea's other side. In fine, a river also is the human mind working in recollection back from ocean into the poet's life. The mind is full of stops, full of remembered latitudes and longitudes of life where the mind's body dwelt for short or longer times and, in the recollections, the mind works back to every kind of source; to every stop along the long, long way until it rests awhile, looks at deep ocean it has ended in and can prepare to face a final door, open the door and sink
below the waves, the ships, the islands ...

Thus *I* must take you from Rhine and Danube, far from yr. native Swabia, to a wider world where sundry rivers run that stopped me in my tracks. I take you to the Thames; the Seine; the Po; the Tiber; Petersburg's Neva and then across old continents over to Ganges; Brahmaputra; an Irrawaddy and a vast Mekong -- drawing at least three countries into their final sea -- then to a Yangtze and a Yellow River; the Baram, the Kinabatangan and the Rajang (Borneo); then down to the Australian Murray and the Darling. And, after this, across to Nile, mother of Egypt, and to Zambezi at Victoria; thus the gigantic falls right there in Africa and tropical Brazil (the Xingu and the Amazon, the Paraná) up through volcano country to the Usumacinta, path of the Maya into my own country, with Mississippi and Missouri and the American-Canadian huge array of falls around, aha! Niagara. Nor does the count stop here. No, not far off, after

my own demise, mankind will sail along the boundless seas of space, finding the Lord alone knows -- should there be a

Lord -- how many rivers, among his countless planets and
the deep stars gone wild beyond all calculation. Did you not
sometimes stop to consider this when looking up at your
sky full of stars still pure, unglazed by so much human light?
To think of it, the stars also have courses up in the oceanic
heavens from which they shine like distant ships carrying
gods backward down to their dwellings -- then humans joy
in their kindness, their tenderness to them while they suffer
the pains of any era and mankind's lack of culture; wisdom;
lack of the means to move with satisfaction into other ways,
other dimensions, with hearts at rest.

A case has to be made on one main point. The poet and the
rivers in his greatest hymns are but a single deed: the demi-
gods that stand between the upper gods and people. Are as
it were *facts* in the determination of what is poetry and what
is people (base: Allemanians and their situation in regards
Greece.) They are *not symbols*, absolutely not: as Mustache,
in his great monograph on "*Ister*" demonstrates. There is a
vast deal more of Mustache when he discusses "homely" and
what the travel from "unhomely" to "homely" means in *Völk-
ish* history: that "homely" cannot occur at all if "unhomely"
does not at first be paramount to his exhausting arguments.
There is far, far too much for my taste on the business V*olk
und Heimat* --- too much indeed with tinges of the dreadful
party swastika. Also a great deal on the "canny" & "uncanny"
in the *Antigone* of Sophocles, a play with great importance to
our hero. The fact that Schelling, Schiller and even Goethe
laughed at his great translations from Sophocles, indeed are
said to have bellowed at them, leaves us in a bad place in re
those senior Germans. They did not dig full transposition of

Greek phrasing into the German language. Voss: "*Ich habe
neulich abends als ich mit Schiller bei Goethe saß, beide recht
dammit regaliert. Lies doch den IV Chor der* Antigone*: Du
hättest Schiller sehen sollen, wie er lachte …*" / "The other eve
I was at Goethe's, also with Schiller, I did amuse them mightily
with it. Try out in reading the IVth Chorus in the *Antigone*: you
should have seen old Schiller laugh!" S. did not answer our own
hero when his great need was greatest and *He* was losing all the
tragic remnants of his fate.

The man with the mustache exhausts one with a constant search
for changing all things into nouns. We poets *now* demand loud,
originary status and the same privilege of masking boundaries
the visual arts and music all enjoy. Our "property"; our "what
is one's own"; we now require -- but on a universal basis -- *that*,
among other goods may find an end to the absurdity of battle.

Translation from one language to another is now so prevalent that the "own languages" cannot be barriers to universal loving recognition. So poets' mothers & fathers; sisters & brothers are in the one truly, the one and only universality. The great among originaries will then remain originaries -- without the masks that scholars hide them with and will continue to be affected by each other. The smaller minors will remain minors enjoying their clear and distinct lack of ability to pay attention to any other minors. Thus on the threshold of twenty thousand years poets will stand and merit recognition at the long last to being "unacknowledged legislators of mankind." Written contrariwise in "Bread & Wine":

> *"Aber Freund! wir kommen zu spät. Zwar leben die Götter,*
> *Aber über dem Haupt droben in andere Welt.*
> *Endlos wirken sie da und scheinens wenig zu achten,*
> *Ob wir leben, so sehr schonen die Himmlischen uns." /*

> "But friend! we have arrived too late. Yes, they live, the gods
> But over our heads, high up, in another world
> There they work, more and more, and seem to care so little
> Whether we live, or do not live." Look & Pray up!

From now on: Duty. All is duty. Breathing is duty. Eating
and passing eating: duty. Moving backward and forward,
sideways at every angle: all is duty. Talking is duty, and
conversation most especially. Shopping is duty, chores
are duty; paying of bills, receiving bills: all this is duty.
Three hours treating the future corpse is duty. No single
thing that can be thought of is not duty. No single thing
that cannot be forgotten on pain of punishment is duty.
Nothing must be forgotten -- or the day is ruined and you
are somehow punished. All work, all composition: Duty.
    Yet duty, truly glimpsed, is Art and nothing else.

It's difficult to be alive and dead at the same time. And
yet an every moment is thus dead and done. All through the
day, your movements do not reach a target worth the name:
every accomplishment, if thus it can be called, falls back
astonished that it could carry through: the energy required
is so malignantly withheld that you could swear your lungs
no longer held the power to decide. No change in world:
that same old music everywhere you tread -- you know
"that song" by heart and it no longer sings for you or hits
or reaches anyone you can still care for. Of all the deaths
inside you the hardest death is love's: as if the memory
were turning into marble and you were trying to cut open
the marble and to recuperate the memory inside. Each day,
each morning you set out into the city, you cannot find the
            path, geography is hidden from you.

The only way to handle it then is to approach as much as
possible, then hope that you will recognize the long known
meeting place between yourself and the attempted tasks
that must be done right there and nowhere else: the food,
the purchases brought home. A recognition and the lack
of it - until you have to meet their eyes that you just barely
know and the apologies pour out: "Of *course* I know you, *I*
have not your name." Babble about an age, a birthday soon

thundering down on you (you do not want it), the aches &
pains. Compulsive. But this is not obsession: this the death
inside you that can no longer care to manifest at every stop.

The tale is told in *His Hyperion* that All is Poetry. A whole
bundle of roles essentially distinctive: in that all are united in
the sin of longing. They long because of drift, of separation:
the *Ur-Teilung,* foul fruit of thought, ill of our consciousness
destructive of the whole, else parting the human from creation.
Through trauma after trauma, the heroes move toward a final
meeting with the "Beloved." It is a story of one last interminable
"arrival" though there is no "arrival." The tale loops round itself
in everlasting circles. The heroes, led by the Titan, heaven's light,
suffer for being present heroes and not the ancient heroes of their
patria -- before the drifts, the separations. Within the present they
cordially detest contemporary life. An ideal "Beloved" is at peace
from the beginning, the incarnation of divine acceptance. *He* goes
therefore, miming into a love-for-two solution: a twin salvation.
"Beloved" weans him back from that toward his destiny on earth.

Meaning that *She* must die. Extinction into Nature did not work.
Return-retreat to childhood did not work. The love-for-two will
neither. "Beloved" sees into *His* heart that *He* is *elegiac* and that
His depths are inconsolable. Ideal, ideal: *He* goes to find in wars,
never achieving a single sprig of peace. Never achieving a sworn
& promised homeland. The driving force is an eternal, unfulfilled,
interminable longing: Nothing will ever satisfy. "*Was mir nicht
Alles, und ewig Alles ist, mir nichts.*" Repudiates the Woman, off
He proceeds to endless war, famished for death. Condemned to fail,
seizing failure. Strong in belief that the ideal is found through loss
and absence. This would be process - in which an overriding scheme,
a harmony is finally achieved. The All-in-One. This *I* believe.

Yet duty to Art continues driving you into yr. home. Art's quiet home.
Its deadly quiet home. You note the sun still moves - and so the moon
desires to join with it. You'll see green hills, green gardens everywhere
traversed by homing rivers: the gods come home with all your fruitful
harvests in their arms. And thus *He* goes, thus the hero's gone. And *She*
departed: *WHEN*? Alive or dead? A question weaves into my bothering:

alive or dead? That star we called our own no longer shines on high: *She* must have died. A cloud passes away, the star's revealed: *She* must yet live. It was a time of glory when we met, when we found twinship in our eyes, our hands moving toward each other, then suddenly: It's never written, cannot be rewritten, but fire devours the whole of earth, leaving just us alone, just holding up a single mountain, the earth's impassioned

hump pointing at sky. Until they came to seize us and to imprison us no, not in walls, not behind bars, but in that death awaited at sundry different times, at different periods. As if we had remembered Oh! life while sick, while fainting far away into a distance. Fate slighting duty.

So let's pretend we are on a vacation. Life's
after all a holiday from death. And death works
  to retrieve us all our lives.

"Wie wenn am Feiertage" / "As on a Holiday"

     "As if on holiday
countryman outs one morning to visit his
own fields: then out of a warm night, deep
cooling flashes fall for hours. Thunder still
noises from a distance; the river falls into
its banks again; new green sprouts from
the soil and the vine drips with joyous rain
while, gleaming in sunlight, our trees stand
    in the grove."

   ***

From out the commentariat, back into poetry.
Celestial light the sign. *He* alone with work:
extreme resolve versus timidity; audacity/
humility; strength/weakness. The birth of
poetry (*Bacchae*: Euripides): Semele, or the
Earth, now impregnated by celestial fire
gives birth to Dionysus. The storm is king:
all recent wars (18th to 19th centuries) bring
on a fundamental change in all divine, all
human lives. Semele struck just as our man
was struck after Bordeaux. Semele turned to
ash: so can our poet pay that price? Yes, at
the end of this, his heart stays firm. However:
what are those last lines about, leaving this
  Hymn unfinished, unfulfilled?

*"So now in this bright weather they all stand:
those whom no master teaches, all in modest
embrace. Miraculously everywhere, god-like
in power and beauty, Great Nature manifests.
So when She seems to sleep at certain times
of year in sky or among plants, or folks, our
poets' faces sadden: they seem to mourn alone
but are always foreboding -- also anticipating
our Great Lady at rest."*

***

Poet has to confront the sacred and emerge
victorious. No mediation. Pure heart, pure
hands. The father's ray is lightning. Sacred
talks to the poet from within the thunder.
The heart is to stand firm. But doubt invades.
The heart bleeds from another arrow: what?
which? The final arrow (arrows bedeck the
work before this Hymn) is not divine: it's
from the man himself. Instead of feeling for
the god who needs a human to feel for him
(*vide "The Rhine"*) the poet suffers from his
own pain and his own weakness. What evil
has he done to his own self?

***

*"But now day's breaking! Waiting I saw it come
--- On what I saw let "Sacred" be my word. For
She herself, She older than the ages and higher
than the gods of East or West, Nature has now
awoken among the clash of armaments and,
from on High, Lord Aether downs to abyssal
pit, according to fixed law, gotten upon as
ever on Holy Chaos. She still, an all-creative,
delights in self-renewal."*

***

It is the poet's fault. The commentator says:
Within the Hymn the menace looks much like
an overconfidence. He thinks that poet has an
ability to face a divine fire. The fact however:
he's feeling insufficient; he goes to the great
dining table of the gods to ask for help. But
goes not as a helper to those gods: he goes in
pain as sufferer. He fears the gods will give
him, like they gave Tantalus, far too much to
digest. And terrified by this he calls himself
"false priest." He is thrown back into the dark
to sing to folks of his anxiety and pain.

***

*"And as a fire lights in that man's eye who has
conceived a high design -- once more by all the
signs, deeds of the world at present, a fire is lit
in the minds of poets. And that which took its
place before but could hardly be felt, manifests
only now. Plus they who smiling worked our
fields for us took on the mien of laborers: they
now are known: the totally alive, the animating
powers of the gods." *

***

In re the terminus of *"Wie & Wenn"*: written
upon the manuscript, in different ink, three
titles: *"Rose," "Swans"* and *"Deer."* Poet cannot
find flowers to make some coronets for those
Celestials. He also chats with swans. There
is a poem *"Die letze Stunde"* later to be called
"A Half of Life." Theme: darkness, loss of love,
loss of the gods. Earth's shadows fail to mediate
twixt sun and earth. Here once again we find the
"Shame on Me!" that ends the poem occur and

peace is lost in *de profundis*. Last words of Hymn
are an abyss: poet must give up on the gods and
know himself broken by wounds he has inflicted
on himself. And thus: since this spells terminus,
     the Hymn can never be completed.

***

"'A Half of Life': With golden pears now
ripe, and fields full of wild roses hanging
down: the country bathing in the lake: oh,
you sweet swans as drunk with kisses you
bend down your heads into the sacred lake …
How sad I am! Where find, when it is winter,
flowers and where's the sun's clarity and
shadows of the earth? The walls stand high and
noiseless in the cold, the wind vanes screech."

***

"And you are asking where they are? In song
their spirit travels when from day's sun and from
warm earth it grows and storms in air and others
more evolved within the depths of time, fuller of
meaning and easier to hear for us, drift on
between heaven and earth and amid the peoples.
They are the thoughts of the communal spirit
and quiet they come down to rest in poets' souls."

***

Another poem now: *"Menons Klagen um Diotima"* /
"Sorrows of Menon in re Diotima": In the first part
the poet, wounded, flees through the forest like a
wounded deer. Goes on to paint a happiness together,
lovers like swans resting beside the lake. Continues
to deplore the lack of song in him, his failure's such
that it's as if he could no longer know ought of the gods.
(There's also talk of the superabundance of the gods'

table poet is longing for.) And thus the ending of the
elegiac vein which poet does not want to take into the
Hymns for then *He* would indeed be that "false priest":
so the unfinished "*Wie & Wenn.*" The wound's the
wound he has suffered himself: the loss of love; he
      thinks was self-inflicted loss of Diotima:

"*Aber das Haus ist öde mir nun, und sie haben mein
Auge Mir genommen, auch mich hab' ich verloren mit
ihr. Darum irr' ich umher, und wohl, wies die Schatten,
so muß ich Leben, und sinnlos dünkt lange das Übrige
mir.*" / "Desolate now is my house and not only *She*
have they taken -- No but my own two eyes! I've lost
myself in losing her. Which is why, lost, I live like ane
wandering phantom lives I fear and all the rest has
      long meant nothing to me."

* * *

"*So that She struck and long familiar to powers
infinite, shaking with recollection and, lit by a holy
radiation, that fruit conceived in love, the work
of gods and men to bear witness to both, the song
succeeds. Once, poets say: When She'd desired
to see the god in person, in the flesh, his lightning
fell onto Semele's house and the divinely struck
gave birth to Holy Bacchus, lord of wine, fruit
      of the thunderstorm.*"

* * *

In the "*Menon/Diotima*" the fates reverse: "Come:
it was like a dream: wings' wounds have healed and
hope leaps out upon the restoration of your youth.
Let those who wish to serve in Orcus serve in the
Underworld, we who were formed by love in silence
will look for the instructions of the gods!" Here is the
state of healing: only the healed can move to the
Celestials. And at the end of "*Wie & Wenn*" our man

is healed having aborted both the imagination and, too, the elegiac. He can then go full-force into the Hymns.

***

"And out of this the sons of Earth without attendant
danger now drink heavenly fire. Yet fellow poets,
we need to stand bareheaded under those thunder
storms to grasp the father's ray, no less, with our
own hands and covering in song the heaven's gift
to give it to our people. For if it happens we are
pure in heart as children and our hands are free,
a father's ray, the pure, will not enflame our hearts
and deeply riven, sharing his sufferings, he stronger
than we are yet in the far-flung, down-rushing storm
of the divine, when he draws near, the heart will find
within itself to stand invulnerable. But ... Oh! my
shame when of

My shame!

And let me say at once

That I approached to see the Heavenly and those
Celestials cast me deep down below the live, into the
darkness down --- And so "false priest" I am to sing
abyssally for those who have no ears to hear
the warning anxious terror of the songs.

There"

The task: to come down from above, bring down, translate,
to suffer through an alienation; from the pure spirit's mind
down to the human heart, (since holy ones feel nothing on
their own, as there can be no movement in them, being in
of themselves perfection - there is no room for any thought,
any volition, to add to what they are already). Thus, they
who move through all the skies, the vacant skies and, since
they have no feet with which to land, interminably floating
through the air, there being not one landing space or limb
with which to land, and were thus known as birds of heaven,
birds of the paradise, ergo they rest down on a human heart,
they take great pleasure in such a dream -- almost as if they
were discovering themselves. And the human heart speaks
what it hears from those who land, breaks these words down
until a unity emerges from the spirit: not a real one, no, just
a sleep, a dream of union, Oh! just the dream perfection's
landed, brought down to earth, a mind discovering that much
has been achieved on earth -- whether to benefit a single soul
or a whole polity! But in reality, as the dream fades along the
push and pull of life: this is illusion, turns out to be illusion,
thus it is recognized -- and thus the product must be dreaming,
the product born of spirit and of mind: there must be longing
here, the reaching out for things dimly imagined as perfection,
of aim achieved, of heaven reached, all the remaining days
so perfect in the light of heaven, in the blue light *He* said, in
the blue light of those who fall into our hearts and mouths,
into our brains, and then go out into the hand and the hand
                   writes, cannot stop writing.

Light on the stairs. The window proves geraniums. And, yes,
a sudden, a life impossible veers into, for some few moments,
a possible. No one can know, except a fellow sufferer, what
the floor means within "depression." Just like the ocean's floor
there's no going below it and there's no lifting it. Brother of
some two hundred years: what did you know exactly? The
knowledge has to leap out -- all at once. What would it mean

to you: One-nine-one-four? One-nine-three-nine? The Hitler
whimper as he held up the gun? The Heideggerian morass as
he gave up his thought ... for a bright badge? But in my case
no, not the mother: the father always. He did not love this *I*.
I did not as he wished. Untrue: he loved but spoke of it to all,
never to self. Mother? *She* always said mother would help but
always, at the very end, took party of the father. Which finally
became pure *nihil*, so often had it been invoked and never used.
And never exercised. *I* thus became pure solitude as a result. *My*
name thus Hyperionides: the god of watchfulness, wisdom and
light ongoing over Earth; (Helios, a son, or he himself: depends
on source). And he, the *I*, who sewed a golden Sun upon his belt
as he came on to his first work one dawn over a Lake he called
"The Lake inside the Sun:" "*Ich bin mir tief bewußt, daß die Sache,
der ich lebe, edel, und daß sie halsam für die Menschen ist.*" / "I
am profoundly conscious the work I live for is a noble work ... one
that is beneficial to mankind."

No one can know how many of the poems were composed within
the folds of a neighbor town after *He*'d left the town of the Beloved.
He had come here, three hours away on foot, to be as close as that.
She'd said "*Wenige sind wie Du*" / "Not many are there like you."
If the whole country had ignored him, at least *She* found him worthy.
He thought abundantly about *His* art and wrote himself interpretations
of that art no one could parse but *He*. *He* wrote no way distracted by
the sadness, *His* "*Hang zur Trauer*," but alongside the sadness, calling
it into poem, transforming spirit into wisdom and entering into *His*
moment in the century, never to be dislodged. Here, for the *I*, there
was a different case since poetry alone could not bring bread -- and
money to buy bread came but reluctantly from *pater*. Was found a way
to love, incorporate the human, though would have been more seemly
to decide for stone -- since stone may speak but never answers back.
Some three decades of work inside the Sun, inside the Lake, listening
to answer-back. Eventually the *Magister* wrote from his deathbed: "I
love, respect the listener, just as I love, respect the writer." Could not
be thanked: died on that note. Loving Gt. Scotsman and Gt. American
(the E. coast one), learned nothing in this world or in the next could be
kept out of song. *I* have such fathers to mask our poverty as we devour
the path.

Aging: catastrophe. Once and for all, away with all the
blather about "Golden Years." This is the face of things
right here. Sunk in interminable pain: pain physical allows
pain mental all the space it needs. Follows desire to bring
an end about: end differs from the quiet cataract into eternal
sleep. Now for difficulties re terminating life. The major
problem involves the other side. Already there's the certainty
there is no knowledge before the life, no knowledge after it.
Whether for normal or voluntary exit: the simple doubt
about departing life is that you'll never know that you have
left it, indeed know anything at all. Was *He*, our lovely *He*,
our foreigner, tempted at any time? An absolute despair of
life's one single love might well have drawn him up into the
crater. Wherein we find the path of *His Empedokles*. There is
a chance *He* might have thought the two of them could die
             together. Letters suggest it.

A Sage Empedokles, thinking himself a poet, caught between
life, death with slumber in-between, believes he has resolved
a crisis of his times. Not just the sin of *hubris*, not just holding
the gods spoke only to himself. Not just figuring out he had not
found the sum of unity in all particulars -- and thus it was all
one whether he lived or died. Not able to persuade his folks that
he could not deliver on his promises -- the gift of endless crops
without devouring storms; the gift of health, well-being, even
happiness (a strange invention granted by gods to unbelieving
mortals); the gift of light from the high realms of spirit, a single
power above the gods leading them through the air into a heaven:
these every failures counted up and measured, there was no point
in staying longer. Above these lacks he felt the failure to hold the
poem, art work, song, the ever *open* ever available to men's eyes
and to decipherment. It made him feel there was no longer sense
in living in his city so up he went on the long path to a volcano's
             crater, not seen, not memorized again.

He had, like certain founders of religions, thought an earth-age would melt and disappear under the powerful foundations such prophets laid in rock, forging a singular new dawn each time into the universe. And thus -- for centuries -- people believed on them and worshiped them devoting vast amounts of time, energy, cash to building temples for them and to the propagation of their word even to those who could not love their faiths -- though force, and empire would at long last persuade them to acceptance. Hero *Empedokles* stands on the rim, the home of fire itself, looks back, and then looks down at his fair earth. In thought, in meditation on the earth, the *I* who'd followed in the fathers' paths recalled his mother's milk, his mother's smile. *I* thinks that, if men could kill these famine-filled religions and give allegiance to one single goddess, the man-made storms, menace to earth's very existence, could, through one mode of labor in devotion, succor the planet. Then the great open field of man's endeavors would at long last live to the very time when planet after planet joined in a marriage dance and all the universe's races could live in endless peace. Out of his memory stood forth the *She*, the goddess *Gaia* accepting at long last this man's devotion to his mother's kind. A rest be history.

When had the future risen up for *I*? When did the break,
the revolutions bloom? Hope and belief in change, Oh ...
just a mere *idea* of revolution? When were the homeless,
hungry, humble people bringing up all hope? They are so
close now! When were the prisons emptied of the slaves?
When did the death penalty - whole barbarism - desist?
When was endemic violence - that bane of deep America
finally violated in a swoop? All guns down-melted now?
When was the population fully educated? ("One Nation ...
under-educated.") When did equality between all peoples,
all sexes, races and beliefs sing out as an ideal? When was
the Great Republic which had initiated glories, definitely
adopted and other nations followed in its wake? When
was a notion of breaking down all borders evaluated up?

There had been France, the Revolution, devotedly beloved
by all *His* friends, waiting to witness its swift coming into
the doors of *His* Germania. Then there had been those foul
and hideous Terrors, a leader falling after all other leaders,
a doubt profound about could this thing last, could it take
over Europe in her stays, that ancient whore? And then, and
then, there is the matter of Napoleon: a brave young general,
thought of at first, who launched his coup to save the French
Republic. Hegel among others, beset by the idea of a novel
religion, saw Nap as acting minus self-understanding and he
himself as understanding Nap. But how to birth a new reality?
If Nap could reach to recognize a Hegel as he had recognized
the Nap, unnecessary duality would be eliminated. Did Hegel
hope, in One Eight O' Six, to be called into Paris? There to

become the Sage of a, yes, universal and homogenic State to
justify and maybe to direct the Nap's activities? Those great
philosophers have ever known temptation! In Hegel's texts:
the result is unclear. But, in any event, the novel's closed and
History is ended. Poor Hölderlin, in this, was a compatriot
fallen in battle: some say the Hegel never thought him "mad."

And this was not the way the Nap believed was Germany's.
Self-proclaimed Emperor, and Empire being One, unique by
definition, the Holy Roman Empire (thus Germanic) just had
to disappear. July One Eighteen O' Six: treaty approved by
sixteen Germanic princes - among them Württemberg, also
Bavaria (now Kings) brought into being that grand assembly:
"Confederation of the Rhine" protected by the Emperor of
the French, signing a peace perpetual and sitting a blank Diet

in Frankfurt city: Höl's place of happiness and torture. Here
was the end of many German hopes albeit the beginning (one
need hardly say) of yet another set. The present frightening.
*He'*d had a past in mind, a golden age. The past was perfect.
It was an ancient land wherein philosophy was born. The *He*
had not been there but had imbibed, with academic milk, its
holy books. *He* ran through them: lands, lakes, rivers and Alps
mountains; cities he would have loved to build again in their
specific places now in ruins; birds, beasts, humans, and gods:
Spirit had lived there, shone in the living daylight, Spirit's son,
Helios illuminating all. All that *He* wrote longed for that past
to shed its light on decimated time *He* and his fellow citizens
lived in at present. Longing is hard, bipolar in some senses: a
past wanted so ardently, the present being paid attention to in

order to bring forth a future for his people. *He* had seen Alps
in a country close to *His*: the massive Swiss looming over a
nation with some freedoms: they were to be the thrones Spirit
would be assigned to when freedom came again through war.
Sunlight would supersede the darkness once again and hope
reborn. *His* poems journeyed through the lands from East to
West, imagining time and again the sacred places and made
their final home in his own country. (Though one might ask:
where was *His* country's Golden Age?) Embedded in that past
now to be overcome: lost love. The loneliness, the sense of
endless wandering, citizenship in doubt, *His* residence in doubt:
own mind's whole sanity in doubt -- and *He* would speak from
high, from visible detachment as if *He* had become a myth or
entered finally God's home. But the relation between the old,

ancient gods and the one God he'd recently pledged once again
allegiance to was now uncertain totally, was moot. What does

poetry do -- except to free the poet? Nothing except to spot the
fiat of one devoted actor. The fiat is a search for lovely meaning
warmed with the science of potential help. No art has ever gone
further than this. As for a coming daylight, new age of happiness:
we have not seen, scarcely believe in it.

Is it lack of the "father?" Is it the missing real, ideal
imaginary, or else symbolic "father"? The "father's
name," i.e., the law, the "father's" missing summons
into the vast symbolic order of mankind (unkind)?
The "father's" no? The "father's" scent of pears in
the lost orchard of his love? Is it among the "real"
First Father: a serene, an image of the *Aether*, that
great god skyward for evermore, or a "real" Second
Father, Magistrate Gock, the kind and gentle? Is it
the great, the worshiped *Meister* Figure, Schiller,
(cities Jena and Weimar), replacement of all "fathers,"
whose love faded away into abandonment? And
even sarcasm? Is it that lord, the worshiped Schiller,
a presence, ever longed for, yet provokes an obscene
sense of a "son's" emptiness? "son's" uselessness? A
leaden hopelessness in him? This object of a triangle
named from an "Oedipus"? As a default or absence of
the "father"? Is horror of "real" Mother, endlessly sad
for two "real" Fathers, holding First Father's money

back from our needy poet? Is it the Mother's endless
will that wishes him to be a curate, oblivious to his
negation of that fate, to his desire impassioned for a
poet's life, his sole desideratum? (Is the poet's turn
into "false priest" asking too much of gods when man, or
woman, could never give enough?) Is he a Son who can
never believe a Mother ever loved him and told her so?

Is it the jealous lover cooling the poet's bliss through cold,
through unavailability, perfection of *Her* being? Is it the
narcissism on the two sides of every love? And a paralysis
of give and take in what can only be closures of passion, of
understanding? Is it the gods, the everlasting "fathers," who
cannot feel but need humans to feel for them, passing at
eagles' height above the universe a poet cares for and staying
above cloud? Is it the pure dissection of a mighty poet tires

this *"I"* so, the disbelief in all those hidden gods that, as for
"I," they cannot hear *His* cries, or bear *His* burdens, grant him
unworldly senses of being cared for -- those that have never
touched humanity in fact but as a grand illusion? Grandest
illusion of human history when *She*, our one and only Dea,
should be our planet *Gaia* whom we should work for day &
night, all days all nights, on pain of losing the only ground
we know, have ever known? On pain of losing Neckar, losing
Danube and Rhine -- all the sacred rivers, gardens and fields,
places our life can signify within, on pain of lost significance
for all, for all those human generations: women, men, poets?

"*In Lieblicher Bläue*" / "In Adorable Blue"

"*In lovely blueness a steeple blossoms over its metal roof.
Around it swallows hover crying, blueness most moving
circling also. Sun, hanging high above, colors its sheet of
tin and above that a weathervane screeches in wind. If
now someone comes down under the steeple bell, comes
down those steps, like a still life: because when figure's so
detached, man's shape's exhibited. Windows from which
bells ring compare with gates in beauty. That is because
those gates conform to Nature still, resembling trees within
a forest. But purity is also beauty. Within, a serious mind
is formed out of diversity. And yet these images so simple,
so very holy, that it is easy to be afraid describing them.
The Heavenly, however, always benign, always all things
at once, just like the rich own such: virtue and pleasure.
This men may imitate. When all of life is hardship, can
man look up and ask: I too would wish to resemble these?
Yes. As long as a pure kindness lasts in his heart man can
compare himself with joy to the divinity. Is God unknown?
Can He be taken for the sky? Yes, I believe this: it is man's
measure.* "Voll Verdienst, doch dichterisch, wohnet der
Mensch auf dieser Erde." / "Deservedly, albeit poetically,
man dwells on Earth." *But a dark night with all its stars is
not more pure, if I can put it so, than man who's called
image of God.*"

"*Is there measure on earth? No, none. For never the Creator's
worlds hold back the thunder's progress. A flower too is full of
beauty because it opens under the sun. The eye, often in life,
discovers beings who could be called more beautiful than
flowers. I know it well! For to bleed both in body and in heart
and wholly to be nothing more than that: would such please
God? Yet I believe the soul must remain pure -- or else the
eagle soars up as far as the Almighty with songs of praise, and
a voice of so many birds. It is the essence and the form. And you,*

you lovely little stream: you are so touching as you flow clear,
clear as the eye divine, right through the Milky Way. I know
you well -- but tears suddenly gush out of my eyes. I see a
life serene encircle me in this creation's shapes because here
I compare it to lonely churchyard doves. But human laughter
sorrows me, for I do have a heart. A comet would I like to be?
I think so. Comets possess bird swiftness, blossom with fire and
seem like children in their purity. To desire more than that, a
human nature cannot presume. Virtue's serenity is also to be
praised by a serious spirit wafting between the garden's triad
of columns. Beautiful virgin must crown her head with myrtle
because she's simple in her nature and her feelings. But myrtles:

they must be sought in Greece."

"If someone looks into a mirror and in it sees his human likeness
as though it were an artist's image: it will resemble him. Man's
image has his eyes, whereas the moon has light. Oedipus Rex
may have an eye too many. His sufferings seem indescribable,
unspeakable and inexpressible. If the play shows up something
like this, that is why. But what comes over me if I think of you
now? Like brooks the end of something sweeps me downstream
and this expands like Asia. Of course this malediction Oedipus
suffers too. Of course that's why. And Hercules as well? Sure.
The Dioscuri in friendship: they suffered too? Because to fight
with God, like Hercules, that is affliction. An immortality in life's
envious heart, to share in that: suffering too. But is this not a
pain as well: to be covered with freckles, wholly covered with
spots! The lovely sun does that which brings up everything. It
leads young men along their chores with the attractions of its
beams as though with roses. The pain Oedipus bore resembles
this as when a poor man's plaint describes a thing he lacks. Sad
son of Laios, stranger in Greece! Life is death; death is a kind

of life."

Solitude creates. Loneliness kills. Takes his last teaching job
as a House-Tutor in Bordeaux, France. *He* writes, "*I am now
full of parting. I have not wept for a long time. But when I
felt I had to leave my country -- perhaps for ever, the tears
became. Oh, they were bitter. For what have I that's dearer in
the world? But they don't have a use for me. I will ever be
German and can't be otherwise, even if my heart's longings
shipped me off to Tahiti for spirit's nourishment.*" Walks to

Bordeaux and back: the job is inconclusive, never described.
He has seen Paris: time for Greek sculpture: Pythian Apollo;
Venus Capitoline, Laocoön. Somewhere it seems *He* meets
with robbers and is bereft. A vision terrible seems to occur:
He writes a friend he has been shattered by no one less than
the Apollo's self "*und wie man Helden nachspricht, kann ich
wohl sagen, daß mich Apollo geschlagen*" / "and as they
say of heroes, I can also say of myself: Apollo's hammered
me." Reaches his home -- that cannot be his home because
of the dread mother -- in a dilapidated, fearsome state. Stays
there two years and yet another half -- his longest homestay
which is not home. Mother reports about him above his head.

Mother and doctors think that writing poems would prevent
cure. What does *He* do? *He* writes a slow march into madness.
The try, the effort is colossal: some days *He* cannot move, not
lift a finger, not write a word. *His* argument: have to write on,
write more and more; so few being achieved. Why does this
writing cost so much more -- in blood & soul? Solitude creates:
No solitude. Loneliness kills: this is not company. *His* likes are
cut from under him, no longer live. Diotima is gone. *He* had a
fury on him when *He* returned: Mother opened his trunk, found
the Beloved's letters, the Diotima's: *He* tried to throw Mother &
Sister out the house. Had gone to see a friend at Stuttgart. And
another friend, Sinclair, his missive forwarded there, caught up
with him: the One Beloved, the Great Beloved *dead solo*. It's
possible (*vide* Bertaux), Susette sent one more letter that was

received after Bordeaux, which caused our H. to go to see her, him coming back in more massive depression as well as taking on blame for her death. This understanding does not treat our H. as "mad" but only existentially depressed -- also accepting role of madman to keep his privacy. This view also suggests a gay Sinclair exasperated by the love saved for Diotima, quarrels with H. and lets him drop. None or but a few accept this.

*"Here is Hyperion, my love, fruit of our days together – when
our souls were at one. Forgive me then for making it so that
Diotima's to die: I thought the disposition of the whole made
it mandatory. Should we admit to one another what's in our
hearts or keep it to ourselves? I have often held back my love
to get through life, this fate of ours. You too who are so kind,
so peaceful, have always struggled to stay calm, have borne
life with heroic strength, kept quiet about things could not be
altered, have hidden buried your Oh! deep heart's decision
within yourself – and for that reason, things may often go dark
around us and we no longer gather who we are and what we
have, and hardly even know one and another. Such endless
conflict and contradiction in the soul, will kill one in the end
and if no god assuages it I have no choice but to grieve into
death away over what's happened to us, or to take nothing to
account excepting you, and look together for a way of ending
this dread conflict ..."*

Loneliness kills. *He* moves in near to Sinclair. Obtains a post
disguised as work in the ducal palace. The writing work has
stopped. Some say not so -- but dates seem to confirm earlier
composition. Someone has gifted him a piano: *He* batters it to
death. No one can breathe him: *"der armer H.; der Narr; ein
wahrer Lumpenhund; ein arme Schlunken"* / "poor H., buffoon,
real ragged mess, pathetic devil." Eventually Sinclair will hand
him back to Mother (first to assign him "mad"), fries other fish.
The loneliness of the great sharks in the warming waters; of the
great elephants in the broiling forests; heat advancing over all the
planet, weather by weather taking its toll on brain, on mind, on
work, the composition. Mountains melt; the rivers overflow and
yet the lakes dry out. Great cities broil. No one can talk; no one
communicate; a sickness spreads in the society at large: the mind
is sick, polluted by destruction; the breaking down of the society;
the failure of the nation. People are daily institutionalized. Cannot
read papers for pollution, cannot watch news at night for constant
pollution. On account nightmare faces of leaders have now become

a counter-solitude, a counter-loneliness: the more they talk, the less they say; the less they are believed. A blight of false politeness born from the violence inbred in this society denies all possibility of true, honest talk. The future looms as terrible as the sad present. There is no present. There's only sickness. A plague, an excremental blight.

More and more people begin to think him "mad." Even some folks *He* had frequented laugh upon hearing some of his work. Even dear friends speak of him as seer -- but yet alas a prophet touched by God. Loss of his post. Friends inattentive on the whole, unconscious of a loss, careless in scattered help. Sinclair announces to the Mother that *He* must be moved. To all intents and purposes, *He*'s kidnapped, sent to a clinic run by a doctor who had invented an anti-screaming mask for lunatics. The clinic's by his one-time college. Students are shown the inmates: *He* is the only lunatic. Insane poet / Sane world? Sane
poet / Insane world? Just calculate!

Thrown out: three years to live the verdict -- given into the care of a good carpenter, a cultured person who knows some of *His* poetry. Z is the name for Zimmer, his house is just below the clinic. Given a room looks over meadows, up in a Tower once part of city walls. Z carpenter and wife, and daughter too (best family his life has ever had) look after his *thirty-six years* of loneliness. A patrimony never spent, the interest has grown: *He* will die rich. And still the family harp on, will bargain with *His* life, shabby manoeuvers are played out. They mess with money, mess with fear that Zimmer's girl, a Lotte, could well become a wife and thus inherit. Zimmer conducts the automatic thank-you letters H. writes unto the Mother. Loneliness kills but not. Excessively polite toward *His* visitors, *He* thus keeps them at bay, *He* will not sign any gift poems with his name, invents some others. One visitor can take him out: feels better in fresh air. On one occasion *He* speaks the name, the one, the only, his "Diotima." *He* lives but fades.

This *His* -- but spoken by the Diotima in an Afterlife --
possibly written midway in the great illness,
conceivably revealing, with a small variant "and/or with kisses"
whether the two were ever lovers in the flesh:
so wonders Christopher, the Middleton:
"*Wenn aus der Ferne*" / "If from the Distance"

"*Forgive me now and think of her who still is glad of that delightful day shone down upon us -- which started with confessions and/or with press of hands and which united us. But Ah! unhappy is that She! Those days were exquisite. However tragic was the dark twilight following after. You are so lonely in this lovely world and so you tell me time after time, my Darling, but, as for that, what you ignore ...*"

There is a break in the work, in the proceedings: one
Feiertag: can you believe it? *I* am immeasurably far
away in the beloved islands, islands adorable, islands
most beautiful in the whole universe. You fly three
hours north of *Tahiti*: it's taken one whole night to
reach Tahiti and you go on from there. *I*'m taking you
to Polynesia, *Ia orana maeva!* No way to get away to
Greece from there; we cannot get to Swabia. A lovely
France in the deep Ocean carries the title of French
Polynesia and France owes it a free and nobler ride:
her independence. What has now journeyed under the
stars? Under the ocean? *I* have a France to love, at
birth known as Great Nation & Great Work, during
our own America's Great War of Independence. My
home in this existence. In *media res*. No other center
to the ocean than this one center multiplied. This is
      the *Internationale* and yet no single nation.

The deep *Marquesas*, Melville's own islands (*I* wrote
in a first book) have arched from out an Eden into
this heart of the Pacific and *I* have traveled with them,
these divine islands. They are both in the center of the
world and north of every place that you can ever think
of. The sea has carried me and *I*'ve been nursed in the
great waters. There's not a single spot in everywhere has
not believed me held in the great waters. Deep in those
woods, the forests of the coastal green, children of fire
and of volcanoes, there is a deeper green, infinitely more
green than any green on earth far from these islands. It is
the place to take some rest, to collect some rest in those
same arms of the deep waters. Off Fatu Hiva. Off Hiva Oa.
Off Nuku Hiva, Ua Huka, Tahuata, Ua Pou, off all desert
and all inhabited, speaking our people's idiom. *Viikona
mahina hei mahina. Puaha te ani. Haa pokeekete ani.
Tai nui. Tai Tokapuha. Hora o te tai.* The language quite
another than the Tahitian. Where is the floor in those deep

seas? Where is the base of world? The ocean dives down into the arms of Sun this time and into sound surrounding, urging you down, sinking you down into the last face of these waters. Sun turns over in a somersault to touch those buried faces of this planet.

Can we talk now a little further while of the relationship, of
the interrelationship Psychosis/Poetry? Of what's Neurosis &
what's Psychosis? Clinical Discourse/Critical Discourse? Only
a little since *I* was never qualified to understand the depths of
Psyche, of its analysis? (And clearly more at home in lit. crit.
speculation: yet not that much - only an anthropologist!) A

workshop made of the life and life's experience, all that to be
devoured, consumed in the work's heart. The work emerges as
life vanishes: a monument.'Twixt life and work language takes
place to totally eat up that work - the *Brennholz* as *He* named
it: a wood for burning. Yet ultimately work must be retrieved
for work alone is life, life insignificant without. In an unending,
immediate brotherhood together with the sacred, *He* veils his
sacred in the silence of the poem so as to calm it down and to
communicate it to mankind. The poet must remain upright, yet
stricken none the less - result: a torn existence in a torn heart

of world. Tension continues. Tension is unavoidable, remains
perpetual. The sickness ("schizophrenia") is life's necessity: a
life's projection at a certain moment, on a certain plane, flaring
perhaps out of a double bind, the point of travel, of trajectory
where truth in its entirety, having become poetic affirmation,
kills off the normal routes of possibility, continues to re-echo,
to reverberate - out of the depths of the impossible as language
"pure," as the "pure word" nearest to undetermined, yet the most
elevated - language unfounded, founded in the abyss - which is
announced also by this one fact: "*the world has been destroyed.*"

This for a man whose greatest question was: How can anything
finite, determined, bear any true relation with an undetermined?
(And what does *I* do if there is no such thing as undetermined?)
If you should ask "Well, is *He* mad?" - this makes the madness
unable to affirm, so much that it could never find a language in
which to speak itself without the threat of madness: language is
mad simply in that it's language. Figures Rhetorical, Poetical &

Metaphorical are defined by some to be specifically Schizoid.
It speaking madness - and thus the poetry is menaced into being
simply "mad language." Ah! such is craziness, this eccentricity
of the poetic language and of its god! The crazy hero Dionysus:
a sudden presence of a god making men mad or making madness
  a plaything of the gods. Recall Semele fried to ashes.

Well: does Psychology come now too close to Kant, Hegel and
Fichte? *He* sees Philosophy, however much *He* reads and writes
it, as a distraction from the poetic task. In fact, *He* once went far
enough, ironically, to call it just a "hospital for our failed poets."
He took Hegel to task especially: H.'s philosophy is *not* to top
and to engulf all discourse: Poetry's total escape is to create a
subject all of its own, in its own right, in its own mastery. Thus
He is not alone a "German Poet" but, as they say, "Poet of Poets."
Takes us two centuries to recognize it and to begin to worship
    at *His* shrine.

The Neckar River. The river *He* was virtually born in.
A river of sweet flowers, trees and birds. Of children.
Below his Tower's window: Tübingen. Two-two-five
miles through Swabia -- now Baden Württenberg and
Hesse. Rises in the Black Forest: Three-one-six feet,
passes through -- of concern to us -- a Nürtingen; and
also Stuttgart, Marbach, Heilbronn, as well as one fine
German glory: my princess Heidelberg: My own, my
very own, where *I* taught once. Discharges well into
the lower Rhine at Mannheim. Between Stuttgart and
Laufen the river cuts a steep-banked course through a
fine valley of Triassic limestone & travertine. Among
the hills sit famous castles. The river's name may owe
to *Nicarus* or *Neccarus* - from Celtic *Nikros* meaning
wild water or wild fellow. And, further down south, so
close together, his two, his wildest rivers: Danube and
Rhine march in opposing courses out of the which the
dialogue is born in his great river Hymns. Re birthing
Nürtingen: first mentioned Ten-four-and-six. Owning
its city rights Thirteen-three-five. Sixteen-three-four:
a population halved by a Thirty Years war and plague.
Seventeen-eighty-three to eighty-four; H. & Schelling
attend the Latin school. Now have the Schellingstrasse,
& Hölderlin Gymnasium. In Nazi times, seventeen labor
camps: some Easterners; some prisoners of war; some
"foreign workers" labor at local companies. A bunch of

children sent out to Auschwitz. The Nazis falsified *Him*.
How can one both love Germany -- and hate it too? One-
nine-four-five: bombs fall on Nürtingen and soldiers flee
through the Tiefenbachtal, a valley south of town. One-
nine-four-eight: the population almost doubles with folks
from Eastern Germany. Still small, still a small rural town.

And there *He* is. *He* is high up, high in the highest sky
unknown to man. His preparations for descent are long

thought-out with his great care. H. was a born skydiver
but a professional never gives up on practice. *He* looks
longingly down. Weary: so over-full of data, *He* thinks:
"No longer have a thought, no longer have my feelings."
And yet *He* comes out of the Sun: a glory round a falling
head --- it's thought *He* is some angel weary of paradise.
He is returning to his home, his long-lost home, dead set
to love it at long last, to live the every minute of every
single day and, yes, to manage in the garden. To raise
an energy to plant new plants at every season. On the top
floor of that, there is the wish *He*'s wished as long as life:
to be a poet, a successful poet, a thing so many, even *His*
family, withheld from him. Remembrances: Come down
my fair Beloved -- from edges of insanity, discover all
possibilities. *She* bound up in *Her* book to give to you, to
you alone of all contemporaries. There is still time. There
will be nearly forty years of time to go on writing. Name
change is quite permissible: Sure! Scardanelli if you like,
or other inconsequent behavior; bizarre modes of address
as you look back from visits into the window of your *Turm*.
Some say you never had been mad. But only wished to be
alone within your purposes. *I*'m fine with that, even if this
outlandish theory will not hold. It would be you all over. It
may have taken years to be invented, to fall into the Neckar.

For, in this love, *I* am as clearly failed as if *I*'d died unfinished:
mind lacking in full sufficiency. *He:* "Thus was I thinking. I'll
say some more about it another time." / "*So dacht' ich. Näch-
stens mehr.*" Life has a thousand cards to play. Death only one.

The following sources were of great use to me in composing this work:

BECK, ADOLF. *Hölderlins Diotima Suzette Gontard: Gedichte, Briefe, Zeugnisse*. Frankfurt am Main: Insel Verlag Taschenbuch 447, 1980.

BERTEAUX, PIERRE. *Hölderlin, ou le temps d'un poète*. Paris: Gallimard, 1983.

BLANCHOT, MAURICE. "La parole 'sacreé' de Hölderlin." *In La Part du Feu*. Paris: Gallimard, 1949.

BLANCHOT, MAURICE. "L'itinéraire de Hölderlin." In *L'Espace Littéraire*, Paris: Gallimard, 1955.

CONSTANTINE, DAVID. *Hölderlin*. Oxford: The Clarendon Press, 1988.

DE MAN, PAUL. *The Rhetoric of Romanticism*. New York: Columbia University Press, 1984.

HARTLING, PETER. *Hölderlin: Biographie*. Translated from the German by Philippe Jaccottet. Paris: Editions du Seuil, 1980.

HEIDEGGER, MARTIN. *Approche de Hölderlin*. Translated by Henry Corbin, François Fédier, Michel Deguy, and Jean Launay. Paris: Gallimard, 1973.

———. *Hölderlin's Hymn "The Ister."* Translated by William McNeil and Julia Davis. Bloomington: Indiana University Press, 1996.

———. *Poetry, Language, Thought*. Translated by Albert Hofstadter. New York: Harper & Row, 1975.

HÖLDERLIN, FRIEDRICH. *Essays and Letters*. Translated with an introduction and notes by Jeremy Adler and Charlie Louth. London and New York: Penguin, 2009.

——— . *Hymns and Fragments*. Bilingual edition. Translated and introduced by Richard Sieburth. Princeton: Princeton University Press, 1984.

——— . *Hyperion and Selected Poems*. Edited by Eric L. Santner. The German Library, vol. 22. New York: Continuum, 1990.

——— . *Poems and Fragments*. Bilingual edition. Translated by Michael Hamburger. London: Routledge & Kegan Paul, 1966.

——— . *Sämtliche Werke und Briefe in fünf Bänden*. Vol. 1, *Gedichte*. Edited by Franz Zinkernagel. Leipzig: Insel Verlag, 1922.

JASPERS, KARL. *Strindberg et Van Gogh: Hölderlin et Swedenborg*. Translated into French from the German by Hélène Naef. With a preface by Maurice Blanchot, "La folie par excellence." Paris: Les Editions de Minuit, 1953.

KRELL, DAVID FARRELL. *The Recalcitrant Art: Diotima's Letters to Hölderlin and Related Missives*. Edited and translated by Douglas F. Kenney and Sabine Menner-Bettscheid. Albany: State University of New York Press, 2000.

LAPLANCHE, JEAN. *Hölderlin and the Question of the Father*. Edited and translated from the French by Luke Carson, with an introduction by Rainer Nägele. Victoria, B.C.: ELS Editions, 2007.

MAYRÖCKER, FRIEDERIKE. *Scardanelli*. Translated from the German by Jonathan Larson. Northampton, MA: The Song Cave, 2018.

MIDDLETON, CHRISTOPHER. *Friedrich Hölderlin: Selected Poems and Letters* (with major essays). Amsterdam: The Last Books, 2019.

SZONDI, PETER. *Poésie et poétique de l'idéalisme allemand*. Translated into French from the German by Jean Bollack with Barbara Cassin, Isabelle Michot, Jacques Michot, and Helen Stierlin. Paris: Editions de Minuit, 1975.

UNGER, RICHARD. *Hölderlin's Major Poetry: The Dialectics of Unity*. Bloomington: Indiana University Press, 1975.

The free-form translations, such as they be, are by myself. All translations are in italics. They only live within *The Hölderliniae* but are insignificant besides the translations of Hamburger, Middleton, Sieburth, Constantine, and a number of others. Fragments from the above texts have sometimes been woven into the work with small, I hope not too reprehensible, alterations.

T. a pris un Nom. Diversité ou Non: Je Maintiendrai.

New Directions Paperbooks — a partial listing

Li Po, Selected Poems
Clarice Lispector, The Hour of the Star
  The Passion According to G. H.
Federico García Lorca, Selected Poems*
  Three Tragedies
Nathaniel Mackey, Splay Anthem
Xavier de Maistre, Voyage Around My Room
Stéphane Mallarmé, Selected Poetry and Prose*
Javier Marías, Your Face Tomorrow (3 volumes)
Bernadette Mayer, The Bernadette Mayer Reader
  Midwinter Day
Carson McCullers, The Member of the Wedding
Thomas Merton, New Seeds of Contemplation
  The Way of Chuang Tzu
Henri Michaux, A Barbarian in Asia
Dunya Mikhail, The Beekeeper
Henry Miller, The Colossus of Maroussi
  Big Sur & the Oranges of Hieronymus Bosch
Yukio Mishima, Confessions of a Mask
  Death in Midsummer
  Star
Eugenio Montale, Selected Poems*
Vladimir Nabokov, Laughter in the Dark
  Nikolai Gogol
  The Real Life of Sebastian Knight
Pablo Neruda, The Captain's Verses*
  Love Poems*
Charles Olson, Selected Writings
Mary Oppen, Meaning a Life
George Oppen, New Collected Poems
Wilfred Owen, Collected Poems
Hiroko Oyamada, The Factory
Michael Palmer, The Laughter of the Sphinx
Nicanor Parra, Antipoems*
Boris Pasternak, Safe Conduct
Kenneth Patchen
  Memoirs of a Shy Pornographer
Octavio Paz, Poems of Octavio Paz
Victor Pelevin, Omon Ra
Alejandra Pizarnik
  Extracting the Stone of Madness
Ezra Pound, The Cantos
  New Selected Poems and Translations
Raymond Queneau, Exercises in Style
Qian Zhongshu, Fortress Besieged
Raja Rao, Kanthapura
Herbert Read, The Green Child
Kenneth Rexroth, Selected Poems
Keith Ridgway, Hawthorn & Child

Rainer Maria Rilke
  Poems from the Book of Hours
Arthur Rimbaud, Illuminations*
  A Season in Hell and The Drunken Boat*
Evelio Rosero, The Armies
Fran Ross, Oreo
Joseph Roth, The Emperor's Tomb
  The Hotel Years
Raymond Roussel, Locus Solus
Ihara Saikaku, The Life of an Amorous Woman
Nathalie Sarraute, Tropisms
Jean-Paul Sartre, Nausea
Delmore Schwartz
  In Dreams Begin Responsibilities
Hasan Shah, The Dancing Girl
W. G. Sebald, The Emigrants
  The Rings of Saturn
Anne Serre, The Governesses
Stevie Smith, Best Poems
Gary Snyder, Turtle Island
Dag Solstad, Professor Andersen's Night
Muriel Spark, The Driver's Seat
  Loitering with Intent
Antonio Tabucchi, Pereira Maintains
Junichiro Tanizaki, The Maids
Yoko Tawada, The Emissary
  Memoirs of a Polar Bear
Dylan Thomas, A Child's Christmas in Wales
  Collected Poems
Uwe Timm, The Invention of Curried Sausage
Tomas Tranströmer, The Great Enigma
Leonid Tsypkin, Summer in Baden-Baden
Tu Fu, Selected Poems
Paul Valéry, Selected Writings
Enrique Vila-Matas, Bartleby & Co.
Elio Vittorini, Conversations in Sicily
Rosmarie Waldrop, Gap Gardening
Robert Walser, The Assistant
  The Tanners
  The Walk
Eliot Weinberger, An Elemental Thing
  The Ghosts of Birds
Nathanael West, The Day of the Locust
  Miss Lonelyhearts
Tennessee Williams, The Glass Menagerie
  A Streetcar Named Desire
William Carlos Williams, Selected Poems
  Spring and All
Louis Zukofsky, "A"

*BILINGUAL EDITION